Autodesk 3ds Max 2019:

A Detailed Guide to Arnold Renderer

Pradeep Mamgain

Autodesk 3ds Max 2019: A Detailed Guide to Arnold Renderer

NOTICE TO THE READER

Examination Copies

Textbooks received as examination copies in any form such as paperback and eBook are for review only and may not be made available for the use of the student. These files may not be transferred to any other party. Resale of examination copies is prohibited.

Electronic Files

The electronic file/eBook in any form of this textbook is licensed to the original user only and may not be transferred to any other party.

Disclaimer

No patent liability is assumed with respect to the use of information contained herein. Although every precaution has been taken in the preparation of this book, neither the author, nor PADEXI, and its dealers and distributors will be held liable for any damages caused or alleged to be caused directly or indirectly by this book. All terms mentioned in this book that are known to be trademarks or service marks have been appropriately capitalized. PADEXI cannot attest to the accuracy of this information. Use of a term in this book should not be regarded as affecting the validity of any trademark or service mark.

Book Code: PDX009P

ISBN: 9781790629800

For information about the books, eBooks, and video courses published by PADEXI ACADEMY, visit our website: www.padexi.academy

Contents

Introduction

Acknowledgments

I would like to express my gratitude to the many people who saw me through this book; to all those who provided support, offered comments, and assisted in the editing, proofreading, and design.

Thanks to:

Parents, family, and friends.

Teachers and mentors: Thank you for your wisdom and whip-cracking--they have helped me immensely.

I am grateful to my many students at the organizations where I've taught. Many of them taught me things I did not know about computer graphics.

Everyone at Autodesk [**www.autodesk.com**].

Finally, thank you for picking up the book.

This page is intentionally left blank

About the Author

I'll keep this short, I am a digital artist, teacher, consultant, and founder of Padexi Academy [**www.padexi.academy**]. I am self-taught in computer graphics, Internet has been the best source of training for me [thanks to those amazing artists, who share the knowledge for free on YouTube]. I have worked with several companies dealing with animation and VFX. I love helping young aspiring 3D artists to become professional 3D artists. I helped my students to achieve rewarding careers in 3D animation and visual effects industry.

I have more than ten years of experience in CGI. I am passionate about computer graphics that helped me building skills in particles, fluids, cloth, RBD, pyrotechnics simulations, and post-production techniques. The core software applications that I use are: Maya, 3ds Max, CINEMA 4D, Photoshop, Nuke, After Effects, and Fusion. In addition to the computer graphics, I have keen interest in web design/development, digital marketing, and search engine optimization.

You can contact me by sending an e-mail to **pradeepmamgain@gmail.com.**

This page is intentionally left blank

Introduction

The **Autodesk 3ds Max 2019: A Detailed Guide to Arnold Renderer** book walks you through every step of rendering projects using Arnold for 3ds Max. This comprehensive guide caters to the novices and intermediate users of Arnold for 3ds Max. This book will help you to get started with Arnold for 3ds Max, you will learn important concepts and techniques about rendering which you can utilize to create high quality renders.

Using a structured and pragmatic approach this guide begins with basics of Arnold, then builds on this knowledge using practical examples to enhance your skills. Each unit builds on the knowledge gained in the previous unit, showing you all the essentials of rendering with Arnold for 3ds Max, from sampling and ray depth, to shaders, maps, camera effects, and AOVs. As you go from hands-on exercise to hands-on exercise you'll develop a strong arsenal of skills that combined will form a complete end to end process to creating high quality renders using Arnold for 3ds Max.

This book shares tips, tricks, notes, and cautions throughout, that will help you become a better 3ds Max rendering artist and you will be able to speed up your workflow. This book is aimed to be a solid teaching resource for learning Arnold for 3ds Max. It avoids any jargon and explains concepts and techniques in an easy-to-understand manner. The first page of the every unit summarizes the topics that will be covered in the unit. Hands-on exercises in this book instruct users how things can be done in Arnold for 3ds Max step-by-step.

Practicing is one of the best ways to improve skills. This book contains practice activities which you are highly encouraged to complete and gain confidence for real-world projects. By completing these activities, you will be able to master the powerful capabilities of Arnold for 3ds Max. By the time you're done, you'll be ready to render any scene in 3ds Max using the Arnold renderer.

*Note: This kindle edition of this book is part of the **kindlematchbook** program. If you buy a new print edition of this book [or purchased one in the past], you can buy the Kindle Edition for FREE. Print edition purchase must be sold by Amazon. If you don't own a Kindle device, you can read the kindle edition with a free Kindle reading app. Visit **https://www.amazon.com/kindle-dbs/fd/kcp** for more information.*

What are the key features of the book?

- The comprehensive guide to learning and using Arnold for 3ds Max.
- Covers all the basics as well as advanced topics using easy to follow, hands-on exercises.
- Explains what is Arnold and how it is different from other renderers.
- Covers Arnold lights and light filters.
- Covers Arnold shaders, materials, and maps.
- Covers the motion blur and depth-of-field effects.
- Covers AOVs and Arnold render settings.
- Detailed coverage of nodes and features.
- Features more than **20** hands-on exercises – complete with before and after files.
- Contains practice activities to test the knowledge gained.
- Additional guidance is provided in the form of tips, notes, and cautions.
- Important terms are in bold face so that you never miss them.
- The content under **"What just happened?"** heading explains the working of the instructions.
- The content under **"What next?"** heading tells you about the procedure you will follow after completing a step(s).
- Includes an ePub file that contains the color images of the screenshots/illustrations used in the textbook. These color images will help you in the learning process. This ePub file is included with the resources.
- Tech support from the author.
- Access to each exercise's initial and final states along with the resources used in hands-on exercises.
- Quiz to assess the knowledge.

Who this book is for?

This comprehensive reference guide not only serves as a reference for intermediate users, but it also easily introduces beginners to Arnold.

What are the prerequisites?

Before jumping into the lessons of this book, make sure you have working knowledge of your computer and its operating system. Also, make sure that you have installed the required software and hardware. You need to install **3ds Max 2019** on your system. Also, install the latest version of Arnold from the Arnold's website [*www.arnoldrenderer.com*]. We have used version **2.2.960** in this book.

How this book is structured?

This book is divided into following units:

Unit A1: Introduction to Arnold, introduces you to the Arnold renderer. You will also learn about the sampling and ray depth settings.

Unit A2: Arnold Lights, introduces you to Arnold lights, light filters, Fog shader, and Atmospheric Volume shader. You will learn about volumetric effects in Arnold.

Unit A3: Arnold Shaders and Materials, explains Arnold materials and shaders.

Unit A4: Arnold Maps, explains the Bump, Color, Conversion, Environment, Math, Shading State, Surface, Texture, User Data, Utility, Volume, and Cryptomatte maps.

Unit A5: Cameras, explains the motion blur and depth-of-field camera effects.

Unit A6: Arnold Render Settings, introduces you to the AOVs in Arnold. You will also learn to create custom AOVs using the AOV write nodes.

Unit PA: Practice Activities, contains practice activities which you are highly encouraged to complete.

Appendix AA: Quiz Answers, contains quiz answers.

Conventions
Icons Used in This Book

Icon	Description
	Tip: A tip tells you about an alternate method for a procedure. It also show a shortcut, a workaround, or some other kind of helpful information.
	Note: This icon draws your attention to a specific point(s) that you may want to commit to the memory.
	Caution: Pay particular attention when you see the caution icon in the book. It tells you about possible side-effects you might encounter when following a particular procedure.
	What just happened?: This icons draws your attention to working of instructions in a hands-on exercise.
	What next?: This icons tells you about the procedure you will follow after completing a step(s).
	Parameter: This icons draws your attention to working of a parameter used in a hands-on exercise.

Given below are some examples with these icons:

Note: Energy Conversion

*Arnold's **Standard Surface** shader is energy conversing by default. In other words, the amount of light leaving does not exceed the amount of incoming light.*

Tip: V-Ray Materials

*You can covert **V-Ray** Materials to **Arnold** materials. A workaround is that you convert V-Ray materials to Autodesk's **Physical** material using the **Universal Material Converter** utility.*

*Then, you can render the **Physical** material within Arnold. This utility can be accessed from the following page: https://www.3dstudio.nl/webshop/product/1-universal-material-converter*

Caution: ActiveShade

*When **ActiveShade** is running, material previews in the material editor are not rendered because only one render session can be active in Arnold.*

Parameters: Density and Density Color

*The **Density** parameter controls the density of the atmospheric volume. The **Density Color** value is multiplied with the value of the **Density** parameter. For example, if you set **Density Color** to red, the red light will be scattered.*

What just happened?

*Here, we have made **Mesh01** emit light in the scene but as you can see in Fig. E2 that light source itself is not visible.*

What next?

*At present, there are no parameters available to make the light source visible using the **Modify** panel. A workaround is to create an emissive **Standard Surface** Arnold material and apply it to the light mesh in the scene. Let's create the material.*

Important Words

Important words such as menu name, tools' name, name of the dialog boxes/windows, button names, and so on are in bold face. For example:

In the **Create** panel, click **Lights**, and then select **Arnold** from the drop-down list below **Lights**. Now, in the **Object Type** rollout, click **Arnold Light**, and then create a light in the scene.

Unit Numbers

Following terminology is used for the unit numbers and appendix:

Unit A1, A2, ... A6: A stands for Arnold.
Unit PA: PA stands for **P**ractice **A**ctivities [Arnold].
Appendix AA: AA stands for Appendix Arnold.

This approach helps us better organize the units when multiple modules are included in a textbook. For example, modeling units will be numbered as **M1, M2, M3**, and so on; the rigging units will be numbered as **R1, R2**, and so on.

Figure Numbers

In theory, figure numbers are in the following sequence **Fig. 1, Fig. 2**, and so on. In exercises, the sequence is as follows: **Fig. E1, Fig. E2**, and so on. In exercises, the sequence restarts from number **E1** for each hands-on exercise.

Naming Terminology

LMB, MMB, and RMB

These acronyms stand for left mouse button, middle mouse button, and right mouse button.

Tool

If you click an item in a palette, toolbar, manager, or window and a command is invoked to create/edit an object or perform some action then that item is termed as tool. For example: **Align** tool, **Mirror** tool, **Select and Move** tool.

Check Box

A small box [labelled as 1 in Fig. 1] that, when selected by the user, shows that a particular feature has been enabled or a particular option chosen.

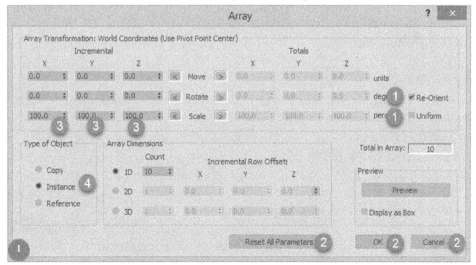

Button

The term button (sometimes known as a command button or push button) refers to any graphical control element [labelled as 2 in Fig. 1] that provides the user a simple way to trigger an event, like searching for a query, or to interact with dialog boxes, like confirming an action.

Dialog Box or Dialog

An area on screen in which the user is prompted to provide information or select commands. Fig. 1 shows the **Array** dialog box.

Spinner

Spinners [labelled as 3 in Fig. 1] are controllers that you will touch on regular basis. They allow you to quickly amend numerical values with ease. To change the value in a spinner, click the up or down arrow on the right of the spinner. To change values quickly, click and drag the arrows. You can also type a value directly in the spinner's field.

Radio Button

A radio button [labelled as 4 in Fig. 1] is the one in which a set of options, only one of which can be selected at any time.

Drop-down

A drop-down (abbreviated drop-down list; also known as a drop-down menu, drop menu, pull-down list, picklist) is a graphical control element, similar to a list box, that allows the user to choose one value from a list. Fig. 2 shows the **Workspaces** drop-down list.

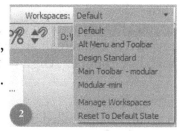

Window

A window is a separate viewing area on a computer display screen in a system that allows multiple viewing areas as part of a graphical user interface (GUI). Fig. 3 shows the **Render Setup** window.

Trademarks

Windows is the registered trademarks of **Microsoft Inc. 3ds Max** is the registered trademarks of **Autodesk Inc.**

Access to Electronic Files

This book is sold via multiple sales channels. If you don't have access to the resources used in this book, you can place a request for the resources by visiting the following link: ***http://www.padexi.academy/contact***.

Fill the form under the **Book Resources [Electronic Files]** section and submit your request.

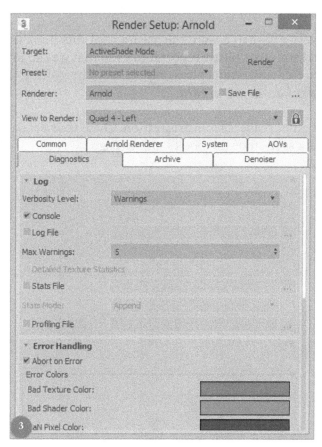

Tech Support

At **PADEXI Academy,** our technical team is always ready to take care of your technical queries. If you are facing any problem with the technical aspect of the textbook, please send an email to author at the following address:
pradeepmamgain@gmail.com

Errata

We have made every effort to ensure the accuracy of this book and its companion content. If you find any error, please report it to us so that we can improve the quality of the book. If you find any errata, please report them by visiting the following link: *http://www.padexi.academy/errata*.

This will help the other readers from frustration. Once your errata is verified, it will appear in the errata section of the book's online page.

- Why Arnold is different?
- What's wrong with the biased algorithms?
- What are the advantages of being physically-based?
- Studio Lighting
- Sampling and Ray Depth

Unit A1: Introduction to Arnold

Arnold developed by Solid Angle [wholly owned subsidiary of Autodesk Inc] is an advanced cross-platform rendering library [API]. Today, it is used by various studios in film, gaming, animation, and broadcast industries across the globe. This unit introduces you to the **MAXtoA** plugin. **MAXtoA** is a plugin for Autodesk 3ds Max which provides a bridge to the Arnold rendering system from within the standard 3ds Max interface.

Arnold was designed to easily adapt to the existing pipelines. It can be extended and customized by writing new shaders, cameras, filters, custom ray types, user-defined geometric data, and so on. The primary goal of the Arnold engine is to provide a complete solution as primary render engine for animation and visual effects projects. However, you can also use it as:

- A ray server for the traditional scanline renderers.
- A tool for creating lightmaps for video games.
- An interactive rendering tool.

 Why Arnold is different?
Here's a quick rundown:

- *It uses highly optimized algorithms to make the most effective use of the computer hardware.*
- *It is physically-based, highly optimized, and photo-realistic.*
- *Its architecture is highly customizable. You can extend and customize it by writing your own shaders, cameras, filters, and so on.*
- *It uses physically-based Monte Carlo ray/path tracing engine thus eliminating the possibility of artifacts [generally produced by the photon mapping and final gather algorithms] produced by the caching algorithms.*
- *It is designed to simplify the production pipeline and renders complex images demanded by VFX studios efficiently.*

- It is used to bake the lighting data to produce lightmaps for video games.
- It is used to as an interactive rendering and relighting tool.

What's wrong with photon mapping or final gather?
To speed up the rendering, these methods attempt to cache the data that can be sampled later. As a result, they consume large amounts of memory and introduce bias into the sampling thus producing artifacts. Also, as a user, they require you to understand the details of how these methods work in order to speed up the rendering without affecting the quality. The worse part of all this is that the settings for these methods get affected by other things in the scene. Arnold allows you to spent time on other aspects of the scene such as modeling, animating, and lighting and it takes care of the rendering.

Why physically-based?
The advantage is that artists can work in a physically accurate and high-range dynamic workflow. It also ensures that other aspects of rendering are not broken.

Note: Downloading plugin
The **MAXtoA** plugin is automatically installed when you installed 3ds Max 2019. However, if a new version is available, you can download it from the Arnold's website: **https://www.arnoldrenderer.com/arnold/arnold-for-3dsmax/** and then install it.

Studio Lighting

Before moving farther, let's first create a photographic lighting studio setup that we will use to render all manner of objects.

Follow these steps:

1. From **Customize** menu choose **Units Setup**. In the **Units Setup** dialog box that appears, select the **Metric** radio button from the **Display Unit Scale** group. Next, select **Centimeters** from the drop-down list located below **Metric** and then click **OK** to accept the changes.

2. From the **File** menu, choose **Save** to open the **Save File As** dialog box. In the **File name** field type **studio-lighting.max** and then click **Save** to save the file.

3. In the **Create** panel, click **Geometry**, and then in the **Object Type** rollout, click **Plane**. In the **Perspective** viewport, create a plane. Switch to the **Modify** panel and then on the **Parameters** rollout, change **Length** to **334**, **Width** to **181**, **Length Segs** to **1**, and **Width Segs** to **1** [see Fig. 1].

4. Convert plane to editable poly and then rename it as **BG**. In the **Modify** panel > **Selection** rollout, click **Edge** to activate the edge sub-object level. Now, select the edge, as shown in Fig. 2. Extrude the edge, as shown in Fig. 3 using **Shift** and the **Move** tool.

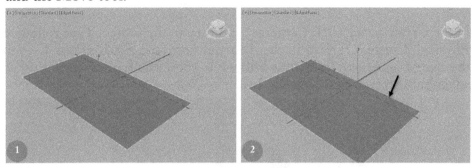

5. Select the middle edge and then in the **Modify** panel > **Edit Edges** rollout, click **Chamfer** > **Settings** to open the **Chamfer** caddy control. In the caddy control, change **Edge Chamfer Amount** to **18** and **Connect Edge Segments** to **4** [see Fig. 4].

6. In the **Create** panel, click **Geometry**, and then in the **Object Type** rollout, click **Plane**. In the **Front** viewport, create a plane. Switch to the **Modify** panel and then in the **Parameters** rollout, change **Length** to **132**, **Width** to **175**, **Length Segs** to **1**, and **Width Segs** to **1**. Now, align the plane [see Fig. 5]. Create a copy of the plane and then align it on the right [see Fig. 6].

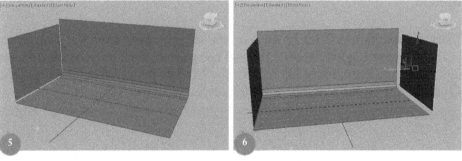

7. Rename the planes as **sidePlane1** and **sidePlane2**, respectively. Group all three planes and name it **Studio**.

8. In the **Create** panel, click **Geometry**, and then in the **Object Type** rollout, click **Sphere**. In the **Perspective** viewport, create a sphere. Switch to **Modify** panel and then in the **Parameters** rollout, change **Radius** to **30** and **Segments** to **64** [see Fig. 7].

9. In the **Create** panel, click **Cameras**, and then in the **Object Type** rollout, click **Physical**. Create a camera in the **Top** viewport [see Fig. 8]. Press **C** to make the camera active and then press **Shift+F** to show safe frames [see Fig. 9]. Now, adjust the camera's view [see Fig. 10].

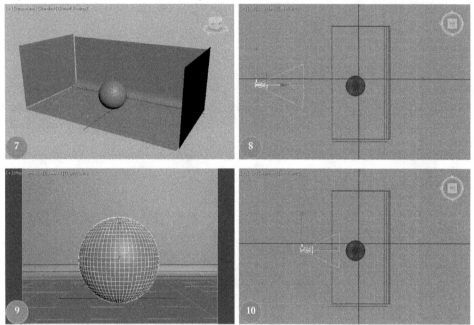

10. Press **F10** to open the **Render Setup** window. In this window, change **Target** to **ActiveShade Mode** and **Renderer** to **Arnold**. In the **Common** panel > **Output Size** group, change **Width** and **Height** to as per your requirements. I recommend that you use low resolution settings for test renders. Close the **Render Setup** window.

11. In the **Create** panel, click **Lights**, and then select **Arnold** from the drop-down list available below **Lights**. In the **Object Type** rollout, click **Arnold Light**. Create a light and then align it [see Fig. 11]. In the **Modify** panel > **Shape** rollout, change **Quad X** and **Quad Y** to **120** and **100**, respectively [see Fig. 12].

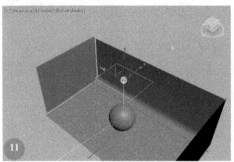

12. Press **M** to open **Slate Material Editor**. Drag **Standard Surface** to active view from the **Material/Map Browser** > **Materials** > **Arnold** > **Surface** rollout. Rename the material as **matBG**. Apply the material to **Studio** in the scene. In **Parameter Editor** > **Specular** rollout, change specular strength to **0** [see Fig. 13].

13. Create a new **Standard Surface** and then rename it as **matObject**. Assign it to the sphere in the scene.

14. Click **ActiveShade** on the **Main** toolbar or press **Shift+Q** to render the scene. Notice in Fig. 14 that render is dark; to fix this either we can increase the **Intensity** or **Exposure** control in the **Modify** panel > **Color/Intensity** rollout > **Intensity** group or we can adjust the camera exposure and f-stop settings. In the **Modify** panel > **Color/Intensity** rollout, change **Exposure** to **9**. Render the scene[see Fig. 15].

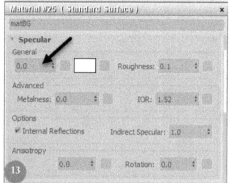

15. Create two more quads lights and align them [see Fig. 16]. Render the scene [see Fig. 17. Notice in Fig. 17 that there is some noise in the render, we will fix it later. Save the scene.

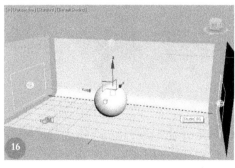

16. Rename lights as **leftLight**, **topLight**, and **rightLight**, respectively. Change **Exposure** setting to **8** for all three lights.

17. Select **leftLight** and then in the **Modify** panel > **Color/Intensity** rollout > **Color** group, select the **Kelvin** radio button and then enter **4000** in the spinner. Similarly, use **12000** as temperature for right light.

Sampling

Arnold is a raytracing renderer. Sampling and ray depth are one of the most important settings for the **Arnold** raytracer. In order to produce a rendered image, Arnold needs to know color value of each pixel. To do so, Arnold fires a number of rays from the camera and then they hit objects in the scene. When rays hit something in the scene, they calculate the information about the surface and return it for processing. This process is called sampling.

The **Sampling** and **Ray Depth** settings are available in the **Render Setup** window > **Arnold Renderer** panel > **Sampling and Ray Depth** rollout [see Fig. 18]. These settings control the sampling [image quality] of the rendered images. Increasing the sample rate removes the noise from the rendered images but at the expense of the increased render time.

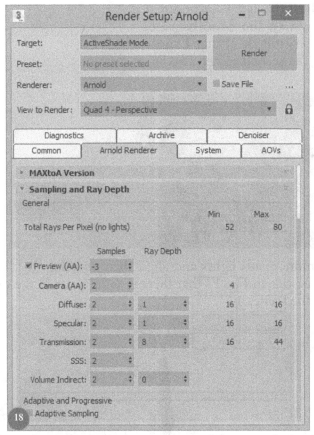

The actual number of samples is the square root of the specified value. For example, if you specify **Camera (AA)** samples as **3** [AA=anti-aliasing], it means that **3x3=9** samples will be used by Arnold for anti-aliasing. If you specify a value of **2** for the **Diffuse** > **Samples**, it means that **2x2=4** samples will be used for global illumination. The same is true for other settings as well.

The **Camera (AA)** setting can be considered global multiplier for all other components: **Diffuse, Specular, Transmission, SSS,** and **Volume Direct** because for these components sampling rates are expressed for each **Camera (AA)** sample.

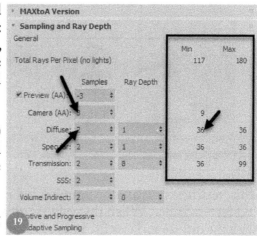

For example, if you specify **Camera (AA)** value as **3** and **Diffuse** as **2**, the total number of samples per pixel used will be **36 [(3*3)x(2*2)]**. Refer to Fig. 19.

Let's now discuss various sampling components:

Preview (AA) Samples

It controls the super-sampling value for previews. It affects the quick first frame before the actual super-sampling starts. The default value for this setting is **-3**. Negative values sub-sample the render therefore allowing faster feedback in the render window.

Camera AA Samples

As discussed earlier, the **Camera (AA)** parameter is global multiplier for all other components. The higher the value you specify for this setting, the better the anti-aliasing quality, and the longer render time will be. In general, use a value of **4** for medium quality, **8** for high quality, and **16** for ultra high quality.

> *Note: Motion blur and depth-of-field*
> *The quality of the motion blur and depth-of-field effects can be improved by increasing the value of the **Camera (AA)** setting.*

Open **studio-lighting-01.max**. Press **F10** to open the **Render Setup** window. In the **Arnold Renderer** panel > **Sampling and Ray Depth** rollout, change **Camera (AA), Diffuse, Specular, Transmission, SSS,** and **Volume Direct** samples to **1** each. Render the scene [see Fig. 20]. Notice that there is lots of noise in the render because we have only used **1** ray-per-pixel.

Now, in the **Render Setup** window, change **Camera (AA)** to **5**. Render the scene [see Fig. 21]. Notice that we are now able to remove substantial amount of noise from the render because of the higher number of AA rays [**5*5=25** rays-per-pixel].

In practice, you will not be using the **Camera (AA)** setting to increase or decrease the quality of the render without paying any attention to other available ray types and the origin of the noise.

Diffuse Samples

This setting controls the number of rays fired when computing the reflected indirect-radiance. When this value is greater than zero, the camera rays intersecting with the diffuse surfaces fire indirect diffuse rays. The diffuse rays are fired in random directions within a hemispherical spread. The noise is introduced when there are insufficient rays to resolve the range of values from the environment. You can increase **Diffuse** samples value to reduce the indirect diffuse noise and improve quality. Fig. 22 is from Arnold website which shows how diffuse rays are propagated in the Arnold render.

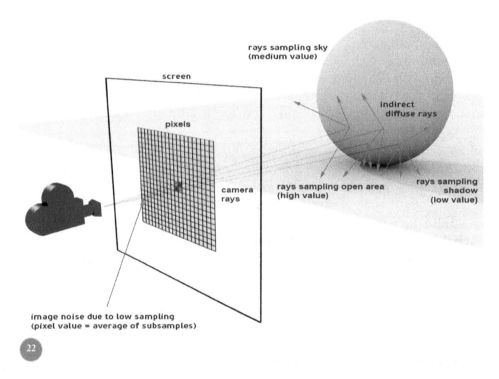

Open **studio-lighting-01.max**. Press **F10** to open the **Render Setup** window. In the **Arnold Renderer** panel > **Sampling and Ray Depth** rollout, change **Diffuse > Samples** to **0** and then render the scene [see Fig. 23]. Notice in Fig. 23 that there is no indirect lighting or global illumination in the scene. The render is only showing the effect of the direct lighting.

In the **Render Setup** window > **AOVs** panel, click **Add AOV File** and then expand **builtin** option in the list. Now, select **diffuse_direct** and **diffuse_indirect** using **Ctrl** and then click **Add** to add the diffuse AOV channels. Render the scene. Fig. 24 shows the **diffuse_direct** channel and Fig. 25 shows the **diffuse_indirect** channel. The render is black because we have set **Diffuse** > **Samples** to **0**.

Change **Diffuse** > **Samples** to **1** and then render the scene; Fig. 26 shows the **diffuse_indirect** channel. The most common cause of noise in a render is due to indirect diffuse noise. It will be more visible in the shadowed areas. Now, we know that the noise in Fig. 26 is indirect diffuse noise Therefore, instead of raising the value of **Camera (AA)** samples, we will raise **Diffuse** > **Samples** samples.

Change **Diffuse** > **Samples** to **5** and render the scene; Fig. 27 shows the **diffuse_indirect** channel. If you compare Fig. 27 with Fig. 26, you will notice that we have quite cleaner result now. Fig. 28 shows the resulting RGBA channel.

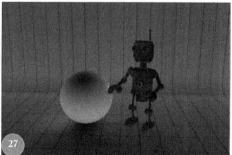

Specular Samples

This setting controls the number of rays fired when computing the reflected indirect-radiance integrated over the hemisphere weighted by a specular BRDF. Fig. 29 from Arnold's website shows how specular rays are propagated in the Arnold render.

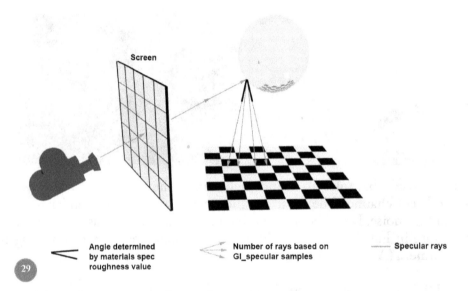

Angle determined by materials spec roughness value	Number of rays based on GI_specular samples	Specular rays

Tip: Noise in specular reflections
*Change the number of **Specular > Samples** to **0** and **Specular > Ray Depth** to **0**. If noise disappears in the render then the noise is due to specular reflections.*

Open **studio-lighting-02.max**. Press **F10** to open the **Render Setup** window. Add the **specular_direct** and **specular_indirect** AOVs. In the **Arnold Renderer** panel > **Sampling and Ray Depth** rollout, change **Camera (AA), Diffuse, Transmission, SSS**, and **Volume Direct** samples to **1** each.

Change **Specular > Samples** to **0** and then render the scene. As expected, the **specular_indirect** channel will render black because there are no samples to calculate indirect specular component. Fig. 30 shows the **specular_direct** channel. Notice in Fig. 30 that the sphere at the left is not appearing in the render because the material applied to it has no specularity.

Change **Camera (AA)** and **Specular** samples to **2** and **5**, respectively. Figs. 31 and 32 show the **specular_direct** and **specular_indirect** channels, respectively.

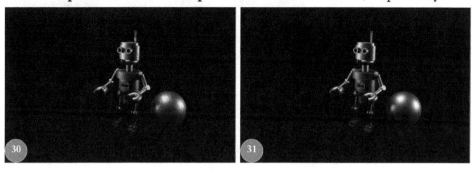

To improve the **specular_direct** pass, we need to increase the light samples. Select **leftLight** and then in the **Modify** panel > **Rendering** rollout, change **Samples** to **4**. Repeat the process for other two lights and then render the scene. Fig. 33 shows the improved **specular_direct** pass.

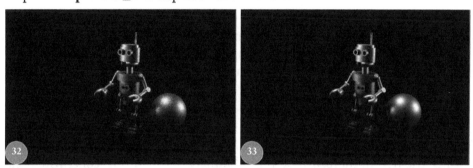

Transmission Samples

This setting controls the number of samples used to simulate the microfacet-based transmission evaluations.

Tip: Noise in transmission
*Change the number of **Transmission** samples to **0** and **Transmission Ray Depth** to **0**. If noise disappears in the render then the noise is due to transmission.*

Open **studio-lighting-03.max**. Press **F10** to open the **Render Setup** window. Render the scene [see Fig. 34]. In the **Arnold Renderer** panel > **Sampling and Ray Depth** rollout, change **Camera (AA)**, **Diffuse**, **Specular**, and **Transmission** to **4, 3, 3,** and **5**, respectively. Render the scene [see Fig. 35].

SSS [Sub Surface Scattering] Samples

This setting controls the number of lighting samples (direct and indirect) that will be taken to estimate lighting within a radius of the point being shaded to compute sub-surface scattering. The higher the values you specify, the cleaner the result be, and the longer the render time will be.

This settings is used to control the number of rays fired to compute the indirect lighting of the volume.

Ray Depth

The **Ray Depth** settings corresponding to the **Diffuse, Specular, Transmission,** and **Volume Indirect** samples allow you to configure settings that limit the ray recursion based on ray type. Higher the value you specify, longer the render time will be. The different ray depth options are discussed next.

Diffuse

The **Diffuse > Ray Depth** parameter controls the diffuse depth bounces. If you set **Diffuse > Ray Depth** to **0**, there will be no diffuse illumination in the scene. On increasing the depth, there will be more bounced light in the scene, which can be especially noticeable in the interior scenes. Figs. 36, 37, and 38 show the render with **Diffuse Ray > Depth** set to **0, 1,** and **2,** respectively. Also, refer to **diffuse-rays.max**.

Specular

The **Specular > Ray Depth** parameter allows you to define the maximum number of times a ray can be glossily reflected. Figs. 39, 40, and 41 show the render with **Specular > Ray Depth** set to **0, 1,** and **2,** respectively. Also, refer to **specular-rays.max**.

Transmission

The **Transmission > Ray Depth** parameter allows you to define the maximum number of times a ray can be refracted. If there are many refractive surfaces in the scene, you may require to use higher ray depth value. Fig. 42 shows the ray depth required for a glass surface with double-sided thickness. Figs. 43, 44, and 45 show the render with **Transmission > Ray Depth** set to **4, 8,** and **16,** respectively. Also, refer to **transmission-rays.max**.

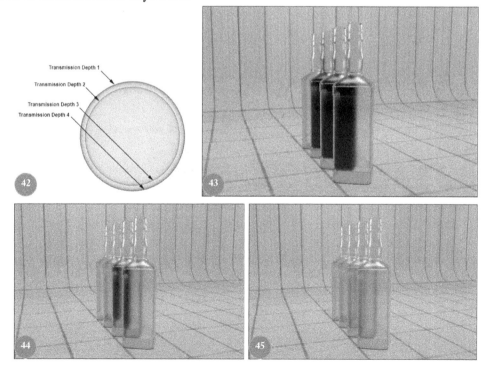

Note: Depth Limits

The options in the **Sampling and Ray Depth** *rollout* > **Depth Limits** *group allow you to set the depth limits for the rays. The* **Ray Limit Total** *parameter specifies the total recursion depth of any ray in the scene. The total rays should be less than equal to the sum of the* **Diffuse**, **Transmission**, *and* **Specular** *rays.*

The **Transmission Depth** *parameter specifies number of allowed transparency hits. When you raise this value, it allows* **Arnold** *to pass more rays through the transparent surfaces. Figs. 46, 47, and 48 show the render with* **Transmission Depth** *set to* **1**, **5**, *and* **14**, *respectively. Also, refer to* **t–depth.max**. *There are six boxes in this scene overlapping each other. The opacity is created using the material's* **Opacity (Cutout)** *parameter. This parameter is available in the* **Special Features** *rollout of the material.*

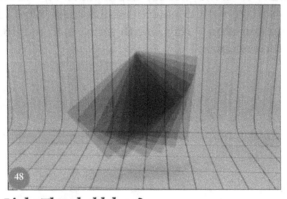

What Low Light Threshold does?

Raising the value of the **Low Light Threshold** *parameter allows to speed up the rendering by not tracing a shadow ray for light samples who contribution is below a certain threshold value. Figs. 49 and 50 shows render with the* **Low Light Threshold** *value set to* **0.13** *and* **0.01**, *respectively. Also, refer to the* **llt.max** *file.*

Volume Indirect

The **Volume Indirect** setting defines the number of multiple scattering bounces within a volume. This is specially useful in rendering large volumes of clouds. Fig. 51 shows the render with the **Volume Indirect** value set to **0** [the default value] and **5**, respectively.

Quiz

Fill in the Blanks

Fill in the blanks in each of the following statements:

1. Arnold uses the physically-based _____ ray/path tracing engine thus eliminating the possibility of artifacts produced by the caching algorithms.

2. The advantage of using physically-based workflow is that artists can work in a physically accurate and _____ dynamic workflow.

3. Arnold is a _____ renderer. _____ and _____ are one of the most important settings for the Arnold raytracer.

4. The _____ samples parameter is global multiplier for all other components.

5. The _____ samples setting controls the number of rays fired when computing the reflected indirect-radiance.

6. The _____ samples setting controls the number of samples used to simulate the microfacet-based transmission evaluations.

7. The _____ parameter allows you to define the maximum number of times a ray can be glossily reflected.

8. The _____ control allows you to define the maximum number of times a ray can be refracted.

True or False
State whether each of the following is true or false:

1. Arnold developed by Solid Angle [a wholly owned subsidiary of Autodesk Inc] is an advanced cross-platform rendering API library.

2. The photon mapping or final gather methods consume large amounts of memory and introduce bias into the sampling thus producing artifacts.

3. Increasing the sample rate does not remove the noise from the rendered images.

4. The **Camera (AA) Samples** value controls the quality of anti-aliasing.

5. The **Specular > Samples** setting defines the number of rays fired when computing the reflected indirect-radiance integrated over the hemisphere weighted by a specular BRDF.

6. The **Diffuse > Samples** setting defines the diffuse depth bounces.

Summary
In this unit, the following topics are covered:

- Why Arnold is different?
- What's wrong with the biased algorithms?
- What are the advantages of being physically-based?
- Studio Lighting
- Sampling and Ray Depth

Unit A2: Arnold Lights

To achieve professional-quality, realistic renders in 3ds Max, you need to master the art of lighting. Lights play an important role in the visual process. They shape the world we see. The trick to simulate realistic looking light effects is to observe the world around us. The lights you create in a scene, illuminate other objects in the scene. The material applied to the objects simulates color and texture.

To access Arnold lights, in the **Create** panel, click **Lights**, and then select **Arnold** from the drop-down list available below Lights [see Fig. 1]. Now, click **Arnold Light** in the **Object Type** rollout; the **Name and Color, General, Shape, Color/Intensity, Rendering, Shadow, Contribution**, and **AOV** rollouts will be displayed.

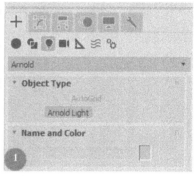

Now, click-drag in a viewport to create a light in the scene.

There are some limitations when using the 3ds Max's **Photometric** lights with Arnold. Here's is the quick rundown of the features not supported by Arnold:

- Some of the light shapes do not support the **Spherical** distribution.
- Only raytraced shadows are supported, rest of the settings are ignored by Arnold.
- The **Exclude/Include** feature is not supported.
- Incandescent lamp-color shift is not supported.
- The light shape is not visible to the camera rays.
- Shadow parameters are not supported.
- The legacy **Atmosphere and Effects** are not supported.

Caution: Exposure Control
The **Physical Scale** value in the **Environment and Effects** window > **Exposure Control** influences the rendering with Arnold lights. In order to get the correct intensity, you need to disable or adjust the **Physical Scale** value to get the expected intensity [refer to Fig. 2].

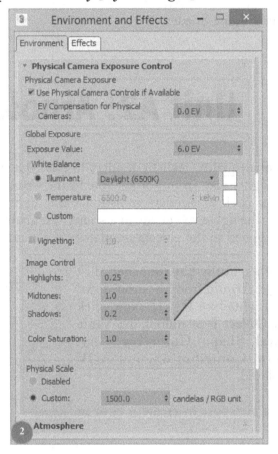

Caution: Constant light decay
The constant light decay feature is not supported in Arnold. However, the **Quad** and **Disk** area lights have a **Spread** parameter that you can use to mimic constant falloff. Similarly, the **Spotlight** type has a **Lens Radius** parameter that you can use along with a low angle to mimic the constant falloff. Another workaround to get constant falloff is to use the distant/directional lighting.

Quad Light

The **Quad** light type simulates light from an area source [refer to Fig. 3]. The source can defined as a quadrilateral specified using four vertices. The following rollouts appear for this light type.

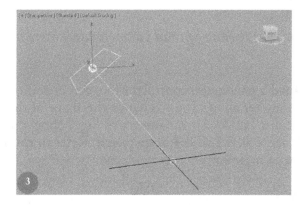

General

The **On** check box is used to toggle the light on/off [refer to Fig. 4]. By default, the **Targeted** check box is selected. As a result, the light will have target object that you can use to point light towards an object. The **Targ. Dist** parameter controls the distance between the light and its target object.

Shape

The options in the **Type** drop-down list are used to select the light type [refer to Fig. 5]. The default light is **Quad**. Other options available are: **Point, Distant, Spot, Quad, Disc, Cylinder, Skydome, Photometric**, and **Mesh**.

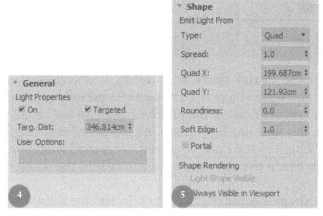

The **Spread** parameter controls the focus of the light in the direction along the normal. The default value for this parameters is **1**. As a result, a diffuse emission of the light is produced. A value of **0** produces a focused laser beam type of emission. The images in Fig. 6 show the render with the **Spread** value set to **0.2, 0.5**, and **1**, respectively. Refer to **spread.max**.

The **Quad X** and **Quad** Y parameters control the four corner points of the quadrilateral. The **Roundness** parameter allows you to change the shape of the light from square [value=**0**, default] to disc [value=**1**]. The images in Fig. 7 show the shape of the light with **Roundness** is set to **0, 0.5**, and **1**, respectively. Refer to **roundness.max**.

The **Soft Edge** parameter controls the smooth falloff for the edges of the light shape. This parameter works similar to the penumbra angle of the spot lights. The images in Fig. 8 show the falloff with **Soft Edge** is set to **1, 0.5**, and **0**, respectively. Refer to **soft-edge.max**.

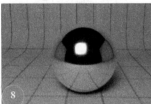  

When you select the **Portal** check box, the light object does not generate any illumination and the light object becomes a light portal. You can use portals with **Skydome** lights to reduce noise in the interior scenes. In such scenarios, light portals are used to guide the skydome light sampling instead of emitting light. In order to guide the samples, light portal must be placed to cover all windows, doors, and other openings through which the skydome light comes into the scene.

When the **Light Shape Visible** check box is selected, the shape of the light is visible as a self-illuminated object in the render. This option is only available for the **Skydome** type. On selecting the **Always Visible in Viewport** check box, the shape of the light will be visible in the viewport even if light is de-selected.

Color/Intensity

The **Color** parameter controls the color emitted by the light. The are some presets available for the light color. You can select them from the **Preset** drop-down list. You can use the **Kelvin** parameter to specify light temperature using Kelvin values. The middle and right images in Fig. 9 shows the render with **Kelvin** value set to **4000** and **12000**, respectively.

The **Texture** parameter can be used to apply a map to the light that will set its color. Fig. 10 shows the render when I connected a HDR map to the **Texture** parameter. Also, refer to the **light-texture.max**. The **Filter Color** parameter allows you to select a color that will be added to the main color of the light.

The **Intensity** parameter controls the brightness of the light source by multiplying the color. The **Exposure** parameter is a f-stop value which multiplies the intensity by $2^{Exposure}$. Therefore, increasing the **Exposure** value by **1** will result in the double the amount of light emitted. The following formula is used for the total amount of light emitted: **Color * Intensity * $2^{Exposure}$**

You can get the same output by either modifying the **Intensity** or **Exposure** value. For example, if you set **Color** to **white**, **Intensity** to **2**, and **Exposure** to **3**; the output will be **16 [1 * 2 * 2^3]**. You can get same output by setting **Intensity** to **16** and **Exposure** to **0** to get output as **16 [1*16* 2^0]**. The **Res. Intensity** label displays the output computed using **Intensity** and **Exposure**.

When the **Normalize Energy** check box is selected, you can control the softness of the shadows changing the size/radius of the light without affecting the amount of emitted light. If you clear this check box, the amount of emitted light is proportional to the surface area of the light.

The images in Fig. 11 show the output with the **Normalize Energy** check box selected and cleared, respectively. The size of the **Quad** light used is **30x30**, refer to **normalize-energy.max**. The images in Fig. 12 show the output with size of the **Quad** light set to **50x50** and **200x200**, respectively. Notice the difference in the softness of the shadows. The **Normalize Energy** check box is cleared in this case.

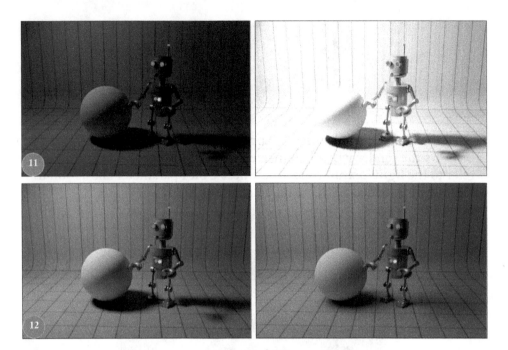

Rendering

The **Samples** parameter controls the quality of the noise in specular highlights and soft shadows. The higher the value you specify, the lower the noise, and the longer it will take to render. The number of shadow rays sent to the light are equal to the square of the value you specify for the **Samples** parameter multiplied by the **AA** samples. The images in Fig 13 show the render with **Samples** set to **1** and **4**, respectively. The **Volume Samples** parameter controls the number of samples used to integrate the in-scattering from direct light. Like the **Samples** parameter it is also a squired value.

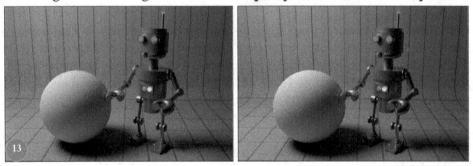

Shadow

The **Cast Shadows** and **Atmospheric Shadows** check boxes allow you enable or disable the computation of the shadow cast from the light and volumetric shadows, respectively. The **Atmospheric Shadows** parameter is not available for the **Distance** and **Skydome** light types.

The **Color** parameter defines the intensity of each color channel for shadows. The **Density** parameter defines the density of strength of the shadows. Normally, you would use a value of **1** which is the default value. The images in Fig. 14 show the strength of shadow with **Density** set to **0, 0.5**, and **1**, respectively.

Contribution

The **Diffuse, Specular, Transmission, SSS,** and **Volume** parameters control the per-light scaling of the diffuse, specular, transparency, sub-surface scattering, and volume components. To produce physically accurate results, the value should be **1** for the contribution. The **Indirect** parameter defines the relative energy loss/gain at each bounce. This parameter should be left at **1** for physically accurate results.

The **Max. Bounces** parameter defines the maximum number of time the energy from the light is allowed to bounce in the scene. A value of **0** will disable global illumination in the scene. This parameter works along with the global ray depth defined in the **Render Setup** window therefore the maximum value of **999** is a theoretical maximum. In practice, the actual ray depth limits are much lower.

When the **Affect Viewport** check box is selected, the light will be used for lighting the scene in the viewport.

 Note: Other light types
*Now, let's explore other light types available in Arnold. The common light parameters have already been discussed in the **Quad Light** section. Following sections describe additional parameters.*

Point Light

The **Point** light type [see Fig. 15] simulates light from a point like a light bulb. Although, the name of the light is **Point** for historical reasons but in practice, a point light is an emissive sphere. The **Radius** parameter defines the radius of the light's spherical radius. If you specify a value of **0** for this parameter then it becomes a true point light with no physical size and it will cast sharp shadows, see Fig. 16.

Distant Light

This light is used to simulate light coming from a distant light source. It is often used to model sunlight. The **Angle** parameter defines the angular size of the Sun. Non-zero values produces realistic looking soft shadows. For example, if you use a value of **1** or **2**, this light will produce slightly soft shadows like produced by hazy sunshine. Higher values like **6** produce much softer shadows.

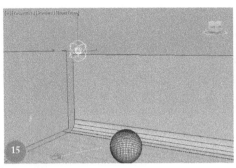 

Spot Light

The **Spot** light [see Fig. 17] simulates light from a spot light. You can use this light to simulate flashlight, a follow spot on a stage, or the headlights of the car.

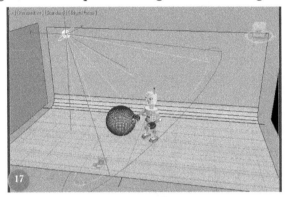

If you set **Radius** to **0**, the cone of light will emanate from a notional point source. With non-zero values, the light source will behave like a spherical source. The radius of the sphere is controlled by the **Radius** parameter. The images in Fig. 18 show the render with **Radius** set to **0**, **2**, and **6**, respectively.

The **Cone Angle** parameter defines the cone angle in degrees. No light can be simulated outside this cone. The **Lens Radius** parameter controls the position of the vertex of the cone. If you specify a value of **0** for the **Cone Angle** parameter, the position of the light coincides with the vertex of the cone.

If value is non-zero, the light come from a virtual position that falls behind the specified position of the light. The images in Fig. 19 show the output when **Lens Radius** is set to **0**, **1**, and **2**, respectively.

The **Penumbra Angle** parameter is measured in degrees from the outer edge of the cone towards the spot light's axis. In the area defined by this parameter, the light's intensity smoothly falls off to zero at the cone edge.

You can use the **Aspect Ratio** parameter to some theater lights such as PAR cans that produce elliptical cross sections. The default aspect ratio of **1** produces circular cross-section. The images in Fig. 20 shows the cross sections with **Aspect Ratio** set to **0.1, 0.3**, and **1**, respectively. Refer to **spot-aspect.max**.

The **Roundness** parameter controls the roundness of the shape of the spot light. The images in Fig. 21 shows the cross sections with **Roundness** set to **0, 0.5**, and **1**, respectively.

Disc Light

The **Disc** light [see Fig. 22] is used to simulate light from a circular area source. The source will always be circular. The **Radius** parameter controls the radius of the disk.

Cylinder Light

The **Cylinder** light [see Fig. 23] is used to simulate light coming from the tube shape objects. The **Radius** parameter is used to increase or decrease the cylindrical light size. The higher the value you specify for this parameter, the larger the area size will be, and the softer the area shadows will be. The **Height** parameter is used to scale the height of the light.

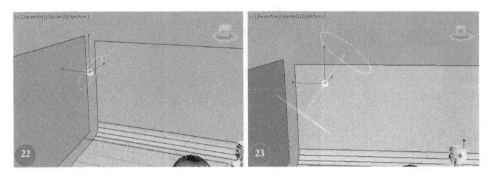

Skydome Light

The **Skydome** light allows you to simulate light coming from a hemisphere or dome above the scene. You can also this light HDR images to simulate image-based lighting. It is specifically used for rendering exterior scenes.

Caution: Interior scenes
*This light specifically suitable for exterior lighting and is represented by a dome above the scene. In interior scenes, most of the trace rays will hit an object. As a result, there will be noise in the render. You can reduce noise by using light portals when using the **Skydome** lighting.*

Note: Environment
*When you add an **Environment** map, **Skydome** light is automatically enabled. As a result, no extra light creation is required. You can specify the environment settings from the **Render Setup** window > **Environment, Background & Atmosphere** rollout.*

The **Resolution** parameter controls the details of reflections on the skydome. For the accurate results, match this value with the resolution of the HDR image. However, in many cases, you can lower the value without a noticeable loss of detail in reflections. The higher the value you specify for this parameter, the longer it will take to precompute the importance table for the light. As a result, scene startup time will increase.

The options in the **Format** drop-down list allow you to select the type of map being connected. The available options are: **Lat-long, Mirrored Ball**, and **Angular**. The options in the **Portal** drop-down list allow you to define how **Skydome** lights interact with the light portals. The following three options are available:

- **Off:** This option disables the portals.
- **Interior Only:** It blocks any light placed outside portals for interior only scenes.
- **Interior/Exterior:** This option lets light outside portals through for mixed interior and exterior scenes.

Tip: Transparent background
*By default, the skydome lights are visible in the background. If you lower the contribution of the camera rays, you will make them invisible. You can lower the contribution by changing the value of the **Camera** parameter in the **Contribution** rollout.*

Caution: Atmosphere Volume Shader
*The **Skydome** light doesn't work with the **Atmosphere Volume** shader. You must use regular lights that have a precise location and size, and the inverse-square decay enabled.*

Mesh Light

The **Mesh** light can be used in the situations where the conventional light shapes are not suffice. Some effects such as neon lighting can be achieved more easily with the **Mesh** light. To assign a geometry to the **Mesh** light, click **None** in the **Shape** rollout > **Emit Light From** group and then click on the geometry on the viewport.

Caution: NURBS Surfaces
*At present, the NURBS surfaces do not work with the **Mesh** lights.*

Caution: Mesh lights and camera rays
*At present, the mesh light is not visible to camera rays. A workaround is create a **Standard Surface** shader and then in the **Parameter Editor** > **Emission** rollout, change emission value to **1**. In the **Base** rollout, change base color strength to **0**. Now, apply this material to the geometry. This workaround will give the impression is that the geometry is incandescent.*

Photometric Light

The **Photometric** lights use data measured from the real-wold lights often provided by the manufacturers themselves. You can import IES profiles from the companies like **Osram** and **Philips**. These companies provide accurate intensity and spread data. To assign a IES file to the light, make sure the light is selected and then in the **Modify** panel > **Shape** rollout, click the browse button corresponding to the **File** parameter and then select the file using the **Select File** dialog box. Refer to Figs. 24, 25, and **photo-light.max**.

Caution: IES Files
*Some of the light manufactures put extra text at the beginning of IES files. If you are facing difficulties in rendering an IES file, open it in a text editor such as **Notepad**. If there is extra text at the beginning, delete it. The file should typically start with **TILT=NONE**.*

Light Filters

Light filters in Arnold are arbitrary shaders that you can use to modify the output of the light based on its distance, position, and other factors. In Arnold for 3ds Max, these filters are available as modifiers. These filters will only be available if you select an Arnold light. The Arnold light filters are discussed next:

Arnold Barn Doors Filter

Barn doors are used in theatrical and film lighting. These are opaque moving panel attached to the sides of the light opening. You can use these doors with Arnold's **Spot** light. When you apply **Arnold Barn Doors Filter** to a **Spot** light, you can access four flaps [**Top**, **Bottom**, **Left**, and **Right**] from the **Modify** panel > **Barn Doors** rollout. Each flap has three parameters [**Top**, **Bottom**, and **Edge**] that you can use to precisely position flaps. Fox example, you can use the **Top Left**, **Top Right**, and **Top Edge** to control the left corner of the top flap, right corner of top flap, and edge softness of the top flap, respectively. Refer to Figs. 26 and 27.

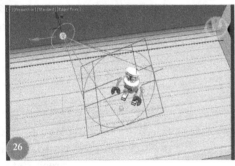

Arnold Gobo Filter

Gobo filters [or cookies] are used in theatrical and film lighting. A gobo is a thin sheet of metal with holes to break up the light beam into an irregular pattern. To apply gobo to a **Spot** light, select it and then from the **Object-Space Modifiers** section of the **Modifier** list, select **Arnold Gobo Filter**. In the **Modify** panel > **Gobo** rollout, assign a map using the **Color** button in the **Slide Map** group and then render the scene to see the effect [refer to Fig. 28 and **gobo-filter.max**]. Any texture map or procedural shader can be projected through the light.

The options in the **Filter** Mode drop-down list allow you to control the blending equation by which the slide map of the gobo is combined with the lights output. **blend** is the default option [refer to Fig. 28]. The images in Fig. 29 show the output with **Filter Mode** to set to **replace, add**, and **mix**, respectively.

The **Density** parameter controls the density of the gobo. The higher the value you specify, the more opaque the gobo will be. The images in Fig. 30 show the output with **Density** set to **0, 0.5**, and **0.75**, respectively.

The **Offset** parameter controls allow you to offset the direction of the texture map. The **Scale S** and **Scale T** parameters are used to scale the map in the **S** and **T** directions, respectively. The **Wrap S** and **Wrap T** parameters control how the texture map is repeated in the **S** and **T** directions, respectively.

Arnold Blocker Filter

Arnold Blocker Filter is a flexible filter that allows you to artificially mask the light beams without adding additional geometry thus giving the artistic freedom. There are four types are blockers available: **box, sphere, plane**, and **cylinder**. You can select the blockers from the **Type** drop-down list available in the **Blocker** rollout > **Properties** group.

Fig. 31 shows the **box** blocker in action [also, refer to **blocker.max**].

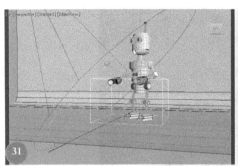 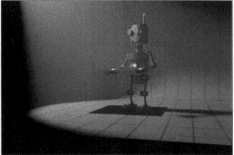

You can control the position, scale, and rotation of the blocker using the parameters available in the **Position**, **Rotation**, and **Scale** groups of the **Blocker** rollout. You can also mask the effect by connecting a texture map with the filter using the parameters available in the **Shader** group. Unlike gobos, you can position a shadow independently of the light transform using **Arnold Blocker Filter** and it works with all lights. Gobos also contribute to the illumination in the scene. However, the shader mask only works if you set **Type** to **box**.

Arnold Decay Filter

By default, all Arnold lights have physically-based falloff. However, if you want to adjust falloff manually, you can use **Arnold Decay Filter**. It allows you to adjust both near and far attenuations. The images in Fig. 32 show the effect of the filter. Also, refer to the **decay-filter.max**.

Hands-on Exercises

Exercise 1: Working with the Mesh Light

In this exercise, we are going to work with the mesh light [see Fig. E1].

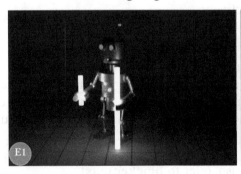 

Table E1 summarizes the exercise.

Table E1	
Topics in this exercise	• Getting Ready • Working with the Mesh Light
Skill Level	Beginner
Time to Complete	20 Minutes
Project Folder	**unit-a2**
Start File	**mesh-light-start.max**
Final Exercise File	**mesh-light-finish.max**

Getting Ready
Open **mesh-light-start.max**.

Working with the Mesh Light
Follow these steps:

1. In the **Create** panel, click **Lights**, and then select **Arnold** from the drop-down list below **Lights**. Now, in the **Object Type** rollout, click **Arnold Light**, and then create a light in the scene.

2. Switch to the **Modify** panel and then in the **Shape** rollout, change **Type** to **Mesh**. Click the **None** button and then click on **Mesh01** in the viewport. Render the scene [see Fig. E2].

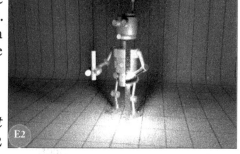

 What just happened?
*Here, we have made **Mesh01** emit light in the scene but as you can see in Fig. E2 that light source itself is not visible.*

 What next?
*At present, there are no parameters available to make the light source visible using the **Modify** panel. A workaround is to create an emissive **Standard Surface** Arnold material and apply it to the light mesh in the scene.*

3. Press **M** to open **Slate Material Editor**. In the **Material/Map Browser > Materials > Arnold > Surface** rollout, drag **Standard Surface** to the active view. In the **Parameter Editor > Base** rollout, set base color strength to **0**. In the **Emission** rollout, set emission strength to **1**. Assign the material to **Mesh01** in the scene.

4. Select light in the scene and then in the **Modify** panel > **Rendering** rollout, change **Samples** to **4**. Render the scene [see Fig. E3].

What next?
*Notice in Fig. E3 that the emissive material is contributing to the diffuse lighting. We need to disable GI bounces for the mesh as the **Mesh** light is already emitting light.*

5. Select **Mesh01** and then from the **Object-Space Modifiers** section of the **Modifier** list, select **Arnold Properties**. In the **Modify** panel > **General Properties** rollout, select the **Visibility** check box and clear the **Diffuse Reflections** check box. Render the scene [see Fig. E4].

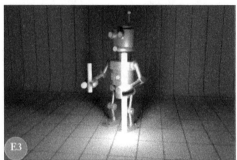

6. Convert **Mesh02** to a mesh light, as discussed above. Render the scene [see Fig. E5].

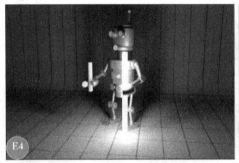

7. Press **F10** to open the **Render Setup** window. In the **Arnold Renderer** panel > **Sampling and Ray Depth** rollout, change **Camera (AA)**, **Diffuse**, and **Specular** samples to 4, 6, and 4, respectively. Render the scene [see Fig. E6].

8. Now, adjust the **Exposure** value to get the output you are looking for.

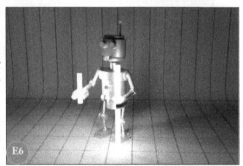

Exercise 2: Working with the Barn Doors Filter

In this exercise, we are going to work with **Arnold Barn Doors Filter** [see Fig. E1].

Table E2 summarizes the exercise.

Table E2	
Topics in this exercise	• Getting Ready • Working with the Barn Doors Filter
Skill Level	Beginner
Time to Complete	20 Minutes
Project Folder	**unit-a2**
Start File	**barn-doors-start.max**
Final Exercise File	**barn-doors-finish.max**

Getting Ready
Open **barn-doors-start.max**.

Working with the Barn Doors Filter
Follow these steps:

1. Select **topLight** and then from the **Object-Space Modifiers** section of the **Modifier** list, select **Arnold Barn Doors Filter**. The barn doors flaps are represented by the blue wireframe at the bottom of the **Spot** light's cone [see Fig. E2].

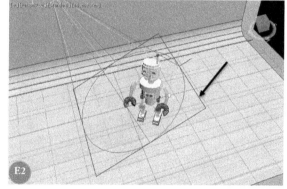

2. In the **Modify** panel > **Barns Doors** rollout > **Top** group, change **Left** to **0.2**.

(?) *What just happened?*
*By increasing the value of **Top > Left**, we have clipped the effect of the light using the top flap from the left side. Refer to Figs. E3 and E4.*

(→) *What next?*
*Now, we will increase the **Top > Right** value to match it with the left value. We will also increase the **Top > Edge** value to soften the effect of the barn doors.*

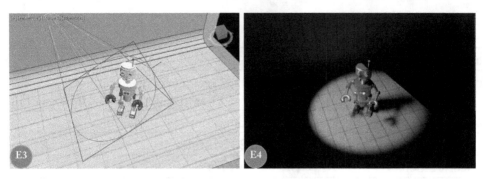

3. In the **Modify** panel > **Barns Doors** rollout > **Top** group, change **Right** to **0.2** and **Edge** to **0.05** [see Figs. E5 and E6].

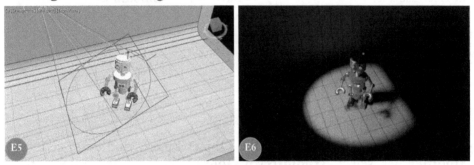

4. Repeat the process for the **Bottom** flap. To match the **Bottom** values with the **Top** values, change **Bottom** > **Left** and **Bottom** > **Right** to **0.8** each [1-0.2=0.8]. Refer to Figs. E7 and E8.

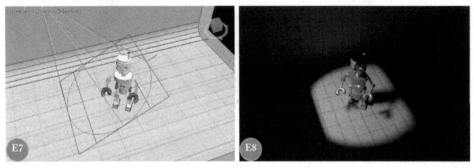

5. In the **Modify** panel > **Barns Doors** rollout > **Left** group, change **Top, Bottom** and **Edge** to **0.2, 0.2**, and **0.05**, respectively.

6. In the **Modify** panel > **Barns Doors** rollout > **Right** group, change **Top, Bottom** and **Edge** to **0.8, 0.8**, and **0.05**, respectively [see Figs. E9 and E10].

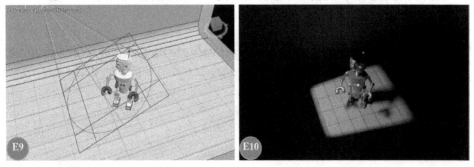

Exercise 3: Working with the Skydome Light

In this exercise, we will illuminate an interior scene using the **Skydome** light [see Fig. E1].

Table E3 summarizes the exercise.

Table E3	
Topics in this exercise	• Getting Ready • Illuminating the Interior Using the Skydome Light • Illuminating the Interior Using Quad Lights
Skill Level	Beginner
Time to Complete	30 Minutes
Project Folder	**unit-a2**
Start File	**interior-start.max**
Final Exercise File	**interior-finish.max** **interior-finish-02.max**

Getting Ready

Open **interior-start.max**. This scene is taken from the Arnold's website. You can download this file and other scene files from the following page:

https://docs.arnoldrenderer.com/display/A5AF3DSUG/Learning+Scenes

Illuminating the Interior Using the Skydome Light

Follow these steps:

1. In the **Create** panel, click **Lights**, and then select **Arnold** from the drop-down list below **Lights**. Now, in the **Object Type** rollout, click **Arnold Light**, and then change **Type** to **Skydome**. Now, click in the viewport to create a light.

2. Select light in the scene and then in the **Modify** panel > **Color/Intensity** rollout > **Intensity** group, change **Intensity** to **1.3** and **Exposure** to **1**. In the **Rendering** rollout, change **Samples** to **4**. Render the scene [see Fig. E2].

3. In the **Shape** rollout > **Shape Rendering** group, select the **Light Shape Visible** check box [see Fig. E3].

What next?
Notice In Fig. E3 that there is lots of noise in the render. Now, we will create three portal lights to guide the **Skydome** samples to the interior to reduce the noise.

4. In the **Shape** rollout, change **Portal Mode** to **Interior** Only.

5. In the **Create** panel, click **Lights**, and then select **Arnold** from the drop-down list below **Lights**. Now, in the **Object Type** rollout, click **Arnold Light**, and then change **Type** to **Quad**. In the **Top** viewport, create the light [see Fig. E4].

6. In the **Modify** panel > **Shape** rollout, change **Quad X** and **Quad Y** to **2341** and **1902**, respectively. Now, align the light [see Fig. E5]. Also, select the **Portal** check box. Create two more instances of the light and align them [see Fig. E6].

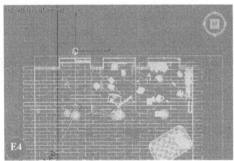
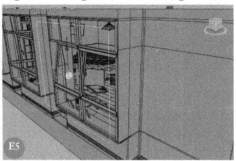

7. Select **Skydome** in the scene and then in the **Modify** panel > **Color/Intensity** rollout > **Intensity** group, change **Intensity** to **0.5** and **Exposure** to **0.8**. Render the scene [see Fig. E7].

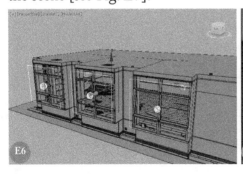

Unit A2: Arnold Lights

8. In the **Create** panel, click **Lights,** and then select **Arnold** from the drop-down list below **Lights.** Now, in the **Object Type** rollout, click **Arnold Light,** and then change **Type** to **Distant.** In the **Left** viewport, create the light [see Fig. E8].

9. In the **Modify** panel > **Color/Intensity** rollout > **Color** group, select the **Kelvin** radio button and then change **Kelvin** value to **4500.** In the **Rendering** rollout, change **Samples** to **4** [see Fig. E9].

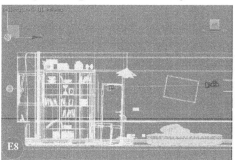

10. Press **F10** to open the **Render Setup** window. In the **Arnold Renderer** panel > **Sampling and Ray Depth** rollout, change **Camera (AA)** and **Diffuse** samples to **5** and **6**, respectively. Also, change **Diffuse > Ray Depth** to **2**. Render the scene [see Fig. E10].

Illuminating the Interior Using Quad Lights
Follow these steps:

1. Press **F10** to open the **Render Setup** window. In the **Arnold Renderer** panel > **Sampling and Ray Depth** rollout, change **Camera (AA)** and **Diffuse Samples** to **3** and **2**, respectively. Also, change **Diffuse > Ray Depth** to **1**.

2. Select the **Skydome** light and then in the **Modify** panel > **Contribution** rollout, change **Diffuse, Specular, Transmission, SSS, Indirect,** and **Volume** to **0.** Render the scene [see Fig. E11]. In the **Shape** rollout, change **Portal Mode** to **Off.**

? *What just happened?*
*By adjusting the contribution values, I have ensured that **Skydome** will be visible to the camera but will not contribute to indirect illumination.*

3. Select one of the portal lights and then in the **Shape** rollout, clear the **Portal** check box. In the **Modify** panel > **Color/Intensity** rollout > **Intensity** group, change **Intensity** to **2** and **Exposure** to **16**. Render the scene [see Fig. E12].

4. Press **F10** to open the **Render Setup** window. In the **Arnold Renderer** panel > **Sampling and Ray Depth** rollout, change **Camera (AA)** and **Diffuse** samples to **5** and **6**, respectively. Also, change **Diffuse** > **Ray Depth** to **2**. Render the scene [see Fig. E13].

Exercise 4: Working with the Image Based Lighting

In this exercise, we will illuminate an exterior scene using the **Skydome** light [see Fig. E1].

Table E4 summarizes the exercise.

Table E4	
Topics in this exercise	• Getting Ready • Illuminating the Scene Using Image-Based Lighting
Skill Level	Beginner
Time to Complete	30 Minutes
Project Folder	**unit-a2**
Start File	**ibl-start.max**
Final Exercise File	**ibl-finish.max**

Getting Ready

Open **ibl-start.max**. This scene is taken from the Arnold's website. You can download this file and other scene files from the following page:

https://docs.arnoldrenderer.com/display/A5AF3DSUG/Learning+Scenes

Illuminating the Scene Using Image-Based Lighting

Follow these steps:

1. Press **8** to open the **Environment and Effects** window. In the **Physical Camera Exposure Control** rollout, clear the **Use Physical Camera Controls if Available** check box and then in the **Global Exposure** group, change **Exposure Value** to **13**.

2. Press **F10** to open the **Render Setup** window. Change **Target** to **ActiveShade Mode** and **Renderer** to **Arnold**. Close the dialog box and then press **Shift+Q** to render the scene [see Fig. E2].

What just happened?
*Here, I have set **Exposure Value** to 13 which is good setting for a daylight scenes. We got dark render because there is no light in the scene and all illumination is coming from the default light.*

3. RMB click on any snap button in the **Main** toolbar to open the **Grid and Snap Settings** dialog box. In the **Snaps** panel, make sure that only the **Grid Points** check box is selected. Close the dialog box and then press **S** to enable snap.

4. In the **Create** panel, click **Lights**, and then select **Arnold** from the drop-down list below **Lights**. Now, in the **Object Type** rollout, click **Arnold Light**, and then change **Type** to **Skydome**. Now, click in the **Top** viewport to create a light. Press **S** to disable snapping.

5. Render the scene; you will notice that the render is too bright [see Fig. E3]. Now, we will decrease the light's exposure to fix it.

6. Make sure light is selected and then in the **Modify** panel > **Color/Intensity** rollout > **Intensity** group, change **Exposure** to 5. In the **Rendering** rollout, change **Samples** to 4. Render the scene [see Fig. E4].

7. In the **Shape** rollout > **Shape Rendering** group, select the **Light Shape Visible** check box, if not already selected. In the **Color/Intensity** rollout, select the **Texture** radio button and then click **No Map** to open **Material/Map Browser**. In the **Maps** > **General** rollout, double-click on **Bitmap** to open the **Select Bitmap Image File** dialog box. Double click on **sky.exr** to open the **OpenEXR Configuration** dialog box. Click **OK**.

8. Render the scene [see Fig. E5].

What Next?
Notice in Fig. E5 that the orientation of the sky is not correct. Next, we will fix it.

9. Make sure that light is selected and then in the **Modify** panel > **Shape** rollout, change **Format** to **LatLong**. Also, change **Resolution** to **2000**. Render the scene [see Fig. E6].

10. Make sure light is selected and then in the **Modify** panel > **Color/Intensity** rollout > **Intensity** group, change **Exposure** to 6. Render the scene [see Fig. E7].

What just happened?
*Notice in Fig. E7 that by increasing the light's **Exposure** value, the sky is not at the correct exposure level. However, the diffuse illumination looks fine. Now, we will fix sky by using the **Contribution** values.*

11. In the **Modify** panel > **Color/Intensity** rollout > **Intensity** group, change **Exposure** to **7**. In the **Contribution** rollout, change **Camera** and **Specular** to **0.25** each. Render the scene [see Fig. E8].

12. Press **F10** to open the **Render Setup** window. In the **Arnold Renderer** panel > **Sampling and Ray Depth** rollout, change **Camera (AA)** and **Diffuse** samples to **5** and **6**, respectively. Render the scene.

Exercise 5: Working with Physical Sky

In this exercise, we will illuminate an exterior scene using **Physical Sky** [see Fig. E1].

Table E5 summarizes the exercise.

Table E5	
Topics in this exercise	• Getting Ready • Illuminating the Scene
Skill Level	Beginner
Time to Complete	30 Minutes
Project Folder	**unit-a2**
Start File	**psky-start.max**
Final Exercise File	**psky-finish.max**

Getting Ready

Open **psky-start.max**. This scene is taken from the Arnold's website. You can download this file and other scene files from the following page:

https://docs.arnoldrenderer.com/display/A5AF3DSUG/Learning+Scenes

Illuminating the Scene
Follow these steps:

1. Press **F10** to open the **Render Setup** window. Change **Target** to **ActiveShade Mode** and **Renderer** to **Arnold**. Close the window.

2. Press **8** to open the **Environment and Effects** window. In the **Physical Camera Exposure Control** rollout, clear the **Use Physical Camera Controls if Available** check box and then in the **Global Exposure** group, change **Exposure Value** to **13**.

3. In the **Common Parameters** rollout, click **Environment Map > None** button to open **Material/Map Browser**. In the **Maps > Arnold > Environment** rollout, double-click **Physical Sky**. Render the scene [see Fig. E2].

> *Note: Physical Sky*
> *The **Physical Sky** shader allows you to implement the **Hosek-Wilkie** sky radiance model in 3ds Max. You can connect it into the 3ds Max's environment or to the **Color** input of the Arnold light. At present, this shader is invisible to **GI Diffuse** and **Specular** rays therefore if you want to use it as a light source, you must attach it to the **Skydome** light.*

4. Press **M** to open **Slate Material Editor** and then drag the **Physical Sky** map from the **Environment and Effects** window into the active view of the material editor as an **Instance**.

5. In the **Parameter Editor > Physical Sky > Parameters** rollout, change **Intensity** to **200**. Render the scene [see Fig. E3].

> *Parameter: Intensity*
> *The **Intensity** parameter value is a scalar multiplier for the sky radiance. This value is similar to the **Sky Tint** value. The difference is that **Sky Tint** uses RGB values whereas it uses scalar values [easier to adjust].*

6. Change **X Axis** to [**1, 0, 0**], **Y Axis** to [**0, 0, 1**], and **Z Axis** to [**0, 1, 0**]. Render the scene [see Fig. E4]. Change **Azimuth** to **215** and **Elevation** to **30**. Render the scene [see Fig. E5]. Change **Sun Size** to **4**.

Parameters: Elevation and Azimuth

*This shader uses polar coordinate system. **Elevation** [sunrise to sunset – measured north to east] has an angle between **0** to **180** degrees whereas the **Azimuth** has an angle [angle of the Sun around horizon] between **0** to **360** degrees.*

Parameter: Sun Size

*The **Sun Size** parameter controls the size of the visible Sun disk. The default value **0.51** is the solid angle of the Sun as seen from the earth. You can increase the size of the disk for artistic purposes. Increasing the value of the **Sun Size** parameter will create softer shadows.*

7. Click on the **Ground Albedo** color swatch to open the **Color Selector** dialog box. Enter **0.5** in the **Value** spinner and click **OK**.

Parameter: Ground Albedo

*This parameter controls the amount of light reflected from earth's surface back into atmosphere. You can use a **RGB** value between **0** to **1** for this parameter.*

8. Change **Azimuth, Elevation, Sun Size, Intensity,** and **Turbidity** to **360, 12, 4, 100,** and **1.5,** respectively.

Parameter: Turbidity

*This parameter determines the amount of aerosol content [dust, moisture, ice, and fog] of the air. This value [range **1** to **10**] affects the color of the Sun and sky. Given below is a quick rundown of the values you can use:*

2: Produces a very clear, arctic–like sky.
3: A clear sky in a temperature climate [default value].
6: A sky on a warm–moist day.
10: A slightly hazy day.

9. Press **F10** to open the **Render Setup** window. In the **Arnold Renderer** panel > **Sampling and Ray Depth** rollout, change **Camera (AA)** and **Diffuse** samples to **4** and **3**, respectively. Render the scene.

 Caution: Fireflies
*Fireflies can appear in the render if you have glass surfaces in the scene and you are using the **Physical Sky** shader to illuminate the scene. This artifacts is caused by the bright Sun disc connected to the background. A workaround is to connect a different **Physical Sky** shader to **Background** that has the **Enable Sun** parameter disabled.*

Exercise 6: Working with the Fog Shader

In this exercise, we will use the **Fog** shader to create the fog in the scene [see Fig. E1].

Table E6 summarizes the exercise.

Table E6	
Topics in this exercise	• Getting Ready • Creating the Fog
Skill Level	Beginner
Time to Complete	30 Minutes
Project Folder	**unit-a2**
Start File	**fog-start.max**
Final Exercise File	**fog-finish.max**

Getting Ready

Open **fog-start.max**. This scene is taken from the Arnold's website. You can download this file and other scene files from the following page:

https://docs.arnoldrenderer.com/display/A5AF3DSUG/Learning+Scenes

Creating the Fog

Follow these steps:

1. Press **F10** to open the **Render Setup** window. In the **Arnold Renderer** tab > **Environment, Background & Atmosphere** rollout > **Atmosphere** group, click the **No Mat** button to open **Material/Map Browser**.

2. In the **Materials > Arnold > Atmosphere** rollout, double-click on **Fog**.

> ✎ *Note: Fog Shader*
> *The **Fog** shader is used in the outdoor environments. It allows you to create effect of light scattering which causes the distant objects to appear in low contrast.*

3. Open **Slate Material Editor** and drag **Fog** material from the **Render Setup** window to the material editor's active view as an **Instance**. Render the scene [see Fig. E2].

4. Click on the **Color** swatch to open the **Color Selector** dialog box. In this dialog box, set **Hue, Sat,** and **Value** to **0, 0, 0.8**, respectively. Render the scene [see Fig. E3].

> ⚙ *Parameter: Color*
> *The **Color** parameter allows you to set the color of the fog. It is recommender that you use unsaturated values for best results.*

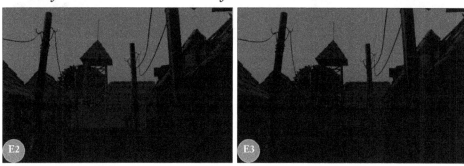

5. Change **Distance** to **0.06** and then render the scene [see Fig. E4]. Change **Height** to **15** and then render the scene [see Fig. E5].

> ⚙ *Parameters: Distance and Height*
> *The **Distance** parameter controls the density of the fog. An exponential distribution is used for the density. The higher the value you specify for this parameter, the denser the fog will be. The **Height** parameter changes the rate of exponential decay along the direction axis. The direction axis is controlled by the **Direction** parameter.*

6. Change **Origin** to **[0, 0, -10]** and make sure **Direction** is set to **[0, 0, 1]**. Render the scene.

Parameter: Origin
*The **Origin** parameter controls the starting point for the fog along the direction axis. The direction axis is controlled by the **Direction** parameter.*

Exercise 7: Working with the Atmosphere Volume Shader

In this exercise, we will use the **Atmosphere Volume** shader to create the atmospheric volume in the scene [see Fig. E1].

Table E7 summarizes the exercise.

Table E7	
Topics in this exercise	• Getting Ready • Creating the Volume
Skill Level	Beginner
Time to Complete	30 Minutes
Project Folder	**unit-a2**
Start File	**vol-start.max**
Final Exercise File	**vol-finish.max**

Getting Ready
Open **vol-start.max**.

Creating the Volume

Follow these steps:

1. Press **F10** to open the **Render Setup** window. In the **Arnold Renderer** tab > **Environment, Background & Atmosphere** rollout > **Atmosphere** group, click the **No Mat** button to open **Material/Map Browser**.

2. In the **Materials > Arnold > Atmosphere** rollout, double-click on **Atmosphere Volume**.

> *Note: Atmosphere Volume shader*
> *You can use the **Atmosphere Volume** shader to simulate light scattered by a thin, uniform atmosphere. This shader is scene–wide volume shader meaning that it will affect all the eligible lights in the scene. This shader works with only the **Point**, **Spot**, and **Quad** lights.*

3. Open **Slate Material Editor** and drag **Atmosphere Volume** material from the **Render Setup** window to the material editor's active view as an **Instance**.

4. In the **Parameter Editor > Atmosphere Volume > Parameters** rollout, change **Density** to **0.02**. Render the scene [see Fig. E2].

5. Click on the **Density Color** swatch to open the **Color Selector** dialog box. In this dialog box, set **Hue**, **Sat**, and **Value** to **0.6**, **0.3**, **0.8**, respectively. Render the scene [see Fig. E3].

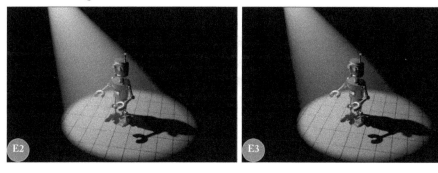

> *Parameters: Density and Density Color*
> *The **Density** parameter controls the density of the atmospheric volume. The **Density Color** value is multiplied with the value of the **Density** parameter. For example, if you set **Density Color** to red, the red light will be scattered.*

6. Change **Attenuation**, **Eccentricity**, and **Samples** to **0.01**, **0.7**, and **8**, respectively. Render the scene.

Parameters: Attenuation, Attenuation Color, Eccentricity, and Samples

The **Attenuation** *parameter controls the rate at which the rays of lights in a scattering medium are extinguished and how much light coming from the background is blocked. The higher the value you specify, the shorter the light travels in the medium. The* **Attenuation Color** *value is multiplied with the value of the* **Attenuation** *parameter. For example, if you set* **Attenuation Color** *to red, the red light will be attenuated.*

The **Eccentricity** *parameter is the* **Henyey-Greenstein** *anisotropy coefficient which ranges from* **-1** *to* **1** *[**full back-scatter** to **full forward-scatter**]. The default value of this parameter is* **0***, which uniformly scatters light in all directions. The positive values bias the scattering in the direction of the light [forward-scatter] whereas the negative values bias the scattering towards the light [backward-scatter]. When you change the* **Eccentricity** *value, the effect generated by light depends on whether the camera is looking toward the light or away from the light. The* **Samples** *parameter defines the quality of the scattering effect.*

 Contribution Parameters

The **Affect Camera**, **Affect Diffuse**, *and* **Affect Reflection** *parameters allow you to control the contribution of the camera rays, diffuse GI rays, and reflection rays, respectively. Non-zero values slow down the rendering speed because the GI rays now need to also do volume calculations.*

 Note: Maps

You can also use maps to affect the scattering effect. You can assign maps from the **Parameter Editor** > **Maps** *rollout of the* **Atmospheric Volume** *shader. For example, you can connect Arnold's* **Noise** *map to the* **Maps** > **Density Color** *parameter to break uniformity in the scattering effect.*

Quiz

Multiple Choice
Answer the following questions, only one choice is correct.

1. Which of the following light types is not available in Arnold?

    [A] Quad   [B] Circle
    [C] Cylinder   [D] Mesh

2. Which of the following filters is available in Arnold?

    [A] Arnold Barns Door   [B] Arnold Gobo
    [C] Arnold Blocker   [D] All of these

Fill in the Blanks
Fill in the blanks in each of the following statements:

1. The _____ light type simulates light from an area source.

2. The _____ parameter controls the focus of the light in the direction along the normal.

3. The _____ and _____ parameters control the four corner points of the quadrilateral.

4. The _____, _____, _____, and _____ parameters control the per-light scaling of the diffuse, specular, sub-surface scattering, and volume components.

5. The _____ shader allows you to implement the **Hosek-Wilkie** sky radiance model in 3ds Max.

True or False
State whether each of the following is true or false:

1. The light portals are used to guide the skydome light sampling instead of emitting light.

2. When the **Light Shape Visible** check box is selected, the shape of the light is visible as a self-illuminated object in the render.

3. You can use the **Temperature** parameter to specify light temperature using **Kelvin** values.

4. The following formula is used for the total amount of light emitted: **Color * Intensity * 2^{Exposure}**

5. The **Ground Albedo** parameter controls the amount of light reflected from atmosphere into earth's surface.

Summary
In this unit, the following topics are covered:

- Arnold Lights
- Limitations of the Arnold Lights
- Light Filters
- Fog Shader
- Atmospheric Volume Shader

- Shaders
- Materials
- Subdivision and Displacement mapping
- Legacy 3ds Max maps

Unit A3: Arnold Shaders and Materials

Arnold supports most of the legacy 3ds Maps such as **Gradient, Noise,** and so on using a feature that calls native C++ maps [not materials]. This feature uses a special Arnold adapter shader.

In order to enable the legacy maps, you need to enable the **Legacy 3ds Max Support** option. To do this, press **F10** to open the **Render Setup** window. Make sure that Arnold is the active renderer. In the **System** tab of the window, select the **Legacy 3ds Max support** check box.

Caution: Legacy 3ds Max support
*Note that this feature only works within **MAXtoA**, it is not supported in the exported **.ASS** files. In some cases, there might be stability issue with **ActiveShade**.*

Here's the list of some of the limitations when using legacy maps with 3ds Max:

- The legacy feature only works within **MAXtoA** because when you use legacy maps, native 3ds Max code is called.
- Since native 3ds Max code is called, you cannot export these maps to an Arnold Scene Source file.
- Everything upstream to a shader must be a 3ds Max shader. Therefore, you cannot use an Arnold shader as input to a 3ds Max shader.
- Every legacy 3ds Max map is not guaranteed to work with Arnold.

Note: Viewport Shaders
*If you use **OSL** maps with **Arnold Surface** shaders, the texture displayed in the viewport will not match the texture displayed in the rendered output because Arnold shaders do not support shader fragments. As a result, the texture are baked before displaying the viewport.*

Caution: ActiveShade
*When **ActiveShade** is running, material previews in the material editor are not rendered because only one render session can be active in Arnold.*

Note: Third-Party Shaders
*Any third-party shader compiled for the current version of Arnold for Windows will work in Arnold. You need to copy the **DLL/MTD/OSL** files to **Plugins/MAXtoA** folder of your 3ds Max installation. Once you copy the files, restart 3ds Max; the shaders will appear in **Material/Map Browser**.*

Tip: V-Ray Materials
*You can covert **V-Ray** Materials to **Arnold** materials. A workaround is that you convert V-Ray materials to Autodesk's **Physical** material using the **Universal Material Converter** utility.*

*Then, you can render the **Physical** material within Arnold. This utility can be accessed from the following page: https://www.3dstudio.nl/webshop/product/1-universal-material-converter*

Note: Supported 3ds Max materials
*The Autodesk's **Physical** material is supported by Arnold. Behind the scenes, 3ds Max translates the material to Arnold's **Standard Surface** material. However, not all features are supported by Arnold. Few material management materials such as **Multi/Sub-Object**, **Blend**, and **Double Sided** as well as pass-through features such as **Direct X Shader**, **Shell Material**, and **XRef** material are supported by Arnold.*

*Other native materials are not supported in Arnold and will render black. If you want to work with some old scenes, use the **Scene Converter** utility to upgrade materials to the **Physical** material.*

Math Shader

Mix Shader

You can use **Mix Shader** to blend two materials. This shader is available in the **Material/Map Browser > Arnold > Math** rollout. You need to use two shaders of the same type such as the **Standard Surface** shader with **Mix Shader**.

To get the output of the **Mix** shader, connect two shaders of same type to the **shader1** and **shader2** ports, respectively. Then, change the blend mode using the **Mode** drop-down list. The **Mix** parameter controls the mix weight [the blending between shaders]. You can also use a map to mix the two shaders using the **Mix** parameter available in the **Maps** rollout. The left image in Fig. 1 shows **shader1**, the middle image shows **shader2**, and the right image shows the output of the **Mix** node. The blending output in Fig. 1 was generated by setting **Mode** to **blend** and specifying a weight of **0.3** for the **Mix** parameter. Also, refer to the **mix-shader.max**.

The left image in Fig. 2 shows the weight map that is used to get the result shown in the right image. Refer to **mix-shader-weight.max**.

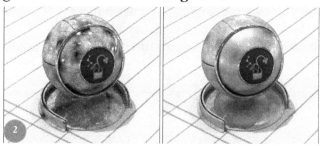

Surface Shaders

Car Paint Shader

The **Car Paint** shader is a simple shader useful for creating car paint materials quickly. Its a layer shader with three layers: **Base**, **Specular**, and clear **Coat**. These layers work similarly to those in the **Standard Surface** shader. However, there are some unique attributes available with the **Car Paint** shader for controlling color ramps and falloff. Also, you can easily add flakes to the specular layer.

In the **Base** rollout, the **Base**, **Base Color**, and **Base Roughness** parameters define the weight, color, and roughness of the primer layer, respectively. The images in Fig. 3 show the result with **Base** set to **0, 0.5**, and **1**. Also, refer to **car-paint.max**.

In the **Specular** rollout, the **Specular** parameter controls the weight of the base coat color. The **Specular Color** parameter defines the color of the specular reflection. It is used to tint the highlight from the base coat layer. The **Specular IOR** parameter controls the index of refraction of the base coat. The **Specular Roughness** parameter controls the glossiness of the base coat layer. The images in Fig. 4 show the result with **Specular IOR** set to **1.5**, **3**, and **6**. Also, refer to **car-paint-specular.max**.

The **Specular Flip Flop** parameter modulates the specular reflection from the base coat depending on the viewing angle. You can connect a **Ramp Rgb** map to this parameter to get the color variation. The images in Fig. 5 show the result with and without the ramp map. Also, refer to **car-paint-flipflop.max**. Fig. 6 shows the ramp.

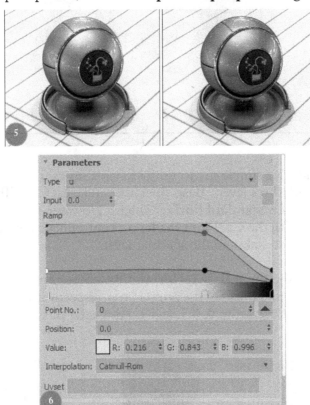

The **Specular Light Facing** parameter modulates the base coat specular color of the area facing the light source. The **Specular Falloff** parameter controls the falloff rate of the light facing color. By specifying a value of **1** for the **Specular Falloff** parameter disables the effect of the **Specular Light Facing** color.

The **Flake Color** parameter in the **Flakes** rollout allows you to tint the specular highlight from flakes. The **Flake Density** parameter controls the density of flakes.

If you a specify a value of **1** for this parameter, the surface will be fully covered with flakes. There will be no flakes if you specify a value of **0** for this parameter. The **Normal Randomize** parameter randomizes the orientation of the flakes. Fig. 7 shows the result with **Flake Density** and **Normal Randomize** parameters set to **0.2** and **1**, respectively. Also, refer to **car-paint-flakes.max**.

The attributes in the **Coat** rollout let you coat the material. The **Coat, Coat Color, Coat Roughness**, and **Coat IOR** parameters control the coat weight, color of the coating layer's transparency, glossiness of the specular reflections, and fresnel reflectivity of the material, respectively.

Lambert Shader

The **Lambert** shader outputs a simple RGB color using the **Simple Lambertian** reflectance model. The **Diffuse, Color**, and **Opacity** parameters control the diffuse weight, diffuse color, and opacity of the material, respectively.

Layer Shader

The **Layer** shader allows you to mix up to eight shaders together. The **Enable** check box is used to enable or disable the layer. You can rename the layer using the **Name** parameter. The **Input [1-8]** expects a surface shader as input. The **Mix [1-8]** parameter controls the blending between the input shaders. The right-most image in Fig. 8 shows the blending of two surface shaders, the left and middle images show the materials that are blended using the **Layer** shader. Refer to **layer-shader.max**.

Matte Shader

The **Matte** shader allows you to create holdout effects by rendering alpha as **0**. The left image in Fig. 9 show the result when the **Matte** shader was applied to the sphere on the left. The right image shows the resulting alpha channel. Refer to **matte-shader.max**.

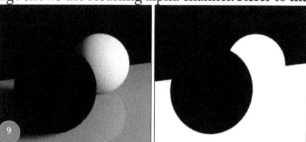

Standard Hair Shader

The **Standard Hair** shader is a physically-based shader that you can use to render hair and fur. This shader is based on the **d'Eon** model for specular and **Zinke** model for the diffuse component. This shader is designed to work with the curve shape node of Arnold and doesn't work on other type of shapes. The **Lambert** shader also work with curves but cannot accurately simulate hair scattering.

To apply this shader, create a **Standard Hair** shader node in the material editor and then select the object. In the **Modify** panel > **Hair and Fur (WSM)** modifier > **Custom** rollout, select the **Apply Shader** check box and connect the **Standard Hair** node.

The intended workflow to connect textures to hair is to set **Melanin** to **0** and then connect texture to the **Base Color** parameter. You can leave **Diffuse** at **0**. In this case, the **Base Color** parameter will affect the secondary specular and transmission component. For accurate results, it is recommended that you don't use the scattering and specular tints parameters found in the **Tint** rollout. These parameters provide antistatic control and therefore are not physically accurate.

The **Base** parameter defines the brightness of the hair, its the multiplier of the base color. The images in Fig. 10 show the result with **Base** set to **0.02, 0.5** and **1**. The **Base Color** was set to RGB **[0.0, 0.141, 0.859]**. Refer to **base-hair.max**.

The **Base Color** parameter defines the color of the hair. This color is absorbed by hair which gives hair its color as light scatters around. You can also connect a texture map to **Base Color** to get variation in the hair color.

 Caution: Bright colored hair
For blond and bright colored hair, a higher number of specular bounces are required to get accurate results.

 Tip: Human hair
*To resemble the appearance of the human hair, it is recommended that you leave **Base Color** as pure white and use the **Melanin** controls to get the plausible colors.*

The **Melanin** parameter lets you control the natural hair colors. It controls the amount of melanin in the hair. You can use a value of **0.2, 0.5**, and **1** for red, brown, and black hair, respectively.

The images in Fig. 11 show the result with **Melanin** set to **0.2, 0.5** and **1**. The **Base Color** was set to pure white and **Melanin Redness** was set to **0.5**. Refer to **base-melanin.max**.

 Tip: Generating hair color using a texture map
If you want to control hair color using a texture, use a value of 0 for the **Melanin** *parameter and then connect the texture to the* **Base Color** *parameter.*

The images in Fig. 12 show the result when texture maps were connected to the **Base Color** *parameter and* **Melanin** *was set to 0. Refer to* **base-color-maps.max**. *The images in Fig. 13 show the maps.*

The **Melanin Redness** defines the redness of the hair. The higher the value you specify for this parameter, the more the proportion of the red **pheomelanin** [found in red hair] will be used relative to the amount of brown **eumelanin**. The **Melanin Randomize** parameter randomizes the amount of melanin in hair fibers.

The **Roughness** parameter in the **Specular** rollout defines the roughness of the hair specular reflections and transmission. Lower values generate sharper and brighter specular highlights whereas higher values generate softer highlights. The images in Fig. 14 show the result with **Roughness** set to **0.2, 0.5** and **1**. Refer to **hair-roughness.max**.

Each fiber of hair is modeled as a dielectric cylinder in Arnold. This fiber reflects and absorbs light depending on the value of the **IOR** parameter. Lower **IOR** values produce strong forward scattering whereas the higher values produce stronger reflection. Fig. 15 show the result with **IOR** set to **1.3, 1.55** and **3**. Refer to **hair-ior.max**.

The **Shift** parameter controls the angle of hair fiber. It shifts the primary and secondary specular reflections away from the prefect mirror detection. For human hair, use a value between **0** and **10** degrees. For synthetic hair, use a value of **0** since the surface of the fiber is smooth. The following table summarizes some of the suggested values.

Table 1: Suggested values for the **Shift** parameter	
Fiber	**Value**
Piedmont	2.8
Light brown European	2.9
Dark brown European	3.0
Indian	3.7
Japanese	3.6
Chinese	3.6
African-American	2.3

Rest of the parameters in **Tint, Diffuse,** and **Emission** rollouts provide additional artistic control but are not required to achieve realistic results.

Note: The Hair & Fur render effect
*To render hair in 3ds Max, the scene must contain a **Hair and Fur** effect. The render effect is automatically added to the scene the first time you apply the **Hair And Fur** modifier to an object. You can access the **Hair and Fur** effect from the **Environment and Effects** window > **Effects** panel [see Fig. 16]. In order to render hair using Arnold, change **Hairs** to **mr prim** from the **Hair and Fur** rollout [refer to Fig. 16] of the **Environment and Effects** window.*

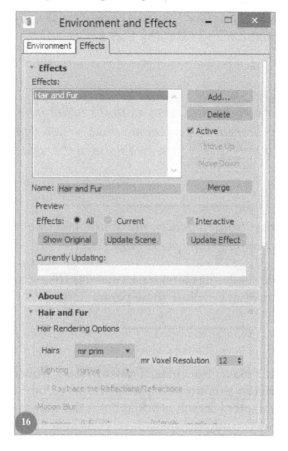

Standard Surface Shader

The **Standard Surface** shader is a physically-accurate shader that you can use to model many types of materials. This material has many layers:

- Diffuse layer
- Specular layer for materials like metals
- Specular transmission layer for materials like glass
- SSS layer for skin
- Thin scattering layer for water and ice materials
- A second layer for specular coat
- A layer for light emission.

By changing few parameters [given below], you can create different materials:

- **Metalness:** Gold, Silver, Iron, Car Paint.
- **Transmission:** Glass, Water, Honey, Soap Bubble.
- **Subsurface:** Skin, Marble, Wax, Paper, Leaves.
- **Thin Walled:** Paper, Leaves, Soap Bubble.

 Note: Energy Conversion
*Arnold's **Standard Surface** shader is energy conversing by default. In other words, the amount of light leaving does not exceed the amount of incoming light.*

 Caution: Layer weights and Colors
*If you use layer weights and colors with the value greater than **1**, the energy conservation is broken. It is recommended that you don't use such weights or colors because it may lead to increased noise in the render and poor rendering time.*

 Caution: Surface normal direction
When rendering diffuse surfaces, make sure that the normals are facing in the right direction to get the predictable results.

The **Standard Surface** shader has lots of parameters. These parameters are grouped under different rollouts. Let's explore these parameters.

Base Parameters

Base Color Group

The first spinner in the **Base, Specular, Transmission, Subsurface, Coat, Sheen, Thin Film,** and **Emission** rollouts is the weight of the corresponding component. The **Base Weight** parameter [default is **0.8**] defines the weight of the base color. The images in Fig. 17 show the output when **Base Weight** set to **0, 0.5,** and **1**.

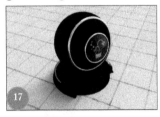  

The **Base Color** parameter defines the base diffuse color. It controls how bright the surface is when lit directly with a white light source with **100%** intensity. The images in Fig. 18 show the output when **Base Color** is set to red, green, and blue. You can also connect maps to the **Base Color** parameter. The images in Fig. 19 show the output with diffuse file textures connected to **Base Color**.

The base component of the shader follows the **Oren-Nayar** reflection model with surface roughness. The **Roughness** parameter allows you to create roughness on the surface. A value of **0** is equal to a **Lambert** reflection, higher values result in rougher surfaces such as concrete, sand, and so on. The images in Fig. 20 show the output with **Roughness** set to **0, 0.5**, and **1** respectively.

Advanced Group

The **Enable Caustics** check box controls whether the specular or transmission bounces behind diffuse bounces are enabled or not. This check box is not selected by default because caustics can be noisy.

Caution: Caustics
*You should take care before selecting the check box because Arnold will need a high number of **Diffuse** samples to achieve a clean result.*

The **Indirect Diffuse** parameter traces a ray against the background/environment when the maximum GI depth [reflection/refraction] is met and return the color of the background/environment in that direction. If you assign a value of **0** to this parameter, the path is terminated and returns black when the maximum GI depth [reflection/refraction] is met.

Specular Parameters

General Group

The **Specular Weight** parameter defines the brightness of the specular highlights. The images in Fig. 21 show the output with **Specular Weight** set to **0, 0.5**, and **1**.

The **Specular Color** parameter tints the color of the reflections. You should only use **Specular Color** for certain type of metals. Non-metallic surfaces do not have a colored specular component. The images in Fig. 22 show the output with **Specular Color** set to red and blue.

The **Roughness** parameter controls the glossiness of the specular reflections. The lower the value you specify, the sharper the reflection. The images in Fig. 23 show the output with **Roughness** set to **0.1**, **0.4**, and **0.6**. You can also use a grayscale map to get the variation in specular highlights. The rougher the surface becomes, the more the reflected light will be blurred.

 Note: Roughness
*The **Roughness** parameter affects both specular reflection and refraction. If you need additional roughness for refraction, you can use the **Extra Roughness** parameter in the **Transmission** rollout > **Advanced** group. If you need to layer the components, you can use the **Coat** layer to create a rough reflection layer over a sharp refraction.*

The **IOR** parameter is used to define the fresnel reflectivity of the material. This value defines the balance between reflections on surfaces facing the viewer and on surface edges. The images in Fig. 24 show the output with **IOR** set to **1**, **1.52**, and **5**.

Caution: Normals

When rendering reflective surfaces, it is very important that the normals are facing in the right direction. Also, it is equally important when rendering single-sided surfaces. The normals should face the outward direction. This is extremely important when rendering surfaces with double-sided thickness, such as glass.

Note: Rendering refraction

*If you see any black where there should be refraction then you may need to increase the **Transmission > Ray Depth** value. The default value is 8 which is sufficient in most of the cases. You can change the **Transmission > Ray Depth** value from the **Render Setup** window > **Arnold Renderer** tab > **Sampling and Ray Depth** rollout.*

The **Metalness** parameter allows you to model a metallic surface. It uses fully specular reflection and complex fresnel. If you want to create prefect sharp mirror-like reflections, set **Metalness** to **1**. The images in Fig. 25 show the output with **Metalness** set to **0, 0.5**, and **1**. The following values are used:

Base Weight: 0.8, **Base Color:** 0.944, 0.776, 0.373
Specular Weight: 0.2, **Specular Color:** 0.998, 0.981, 0.751

The metal appearance is controlled by the **Base Color** and **Specular Color** parameters. The **Base Color** parameter controls the facing color whereas the **Specular Color** parameter controls the edge tint.

Note: IOR and Metalness

*You should normally use **IOR** for materials like plastic, glass, or skin [dielectric fresnel] and **Metalness** for metals [conductive fresnel with Complex IOR]. Using a very high **IOR** value can look quite similar to **Metalness**. The **Metalness** is easy to control as it ranges from **0** to **1**.*

Tip: PBR metalness map

*If you use **Substance Painter**, you can create a metalness map from it and connect it to the **Metalness** parameter.*

Options Group

If you clear the **Internal Reflections** check box, Arnold will disable indirect specular and mirror perfect reflection computations when ray refraction depth is bigger than

0. The **Indirect Specular** parameter controls the amount of specularity received from the indirect sources. It scales the indirect specular component. If you use any value other than **1**, the material will not follow energy preservation.

Anisotropy Group

The **Specular Anisotropy** value reflects the light with a directional bias and causes the material to be rougher or glossier in certain directions. The higher the value you specify, the more pronounced the anisotropic reflectance will be. The images in Fig. 26 show the output with **Specular Anisotropy** set to **0, 0.5,** and **1**. Refer to the **anisotropy.max** file.

Caution: Faceting in Specular Highlights
*You may notice faceting appear in the specular highlights [see left image in Fig. 27]. To fix it, you can enable smooth subdivision tangents. Also, this requires a subdivision iteration of at least **1** in the geometry. To fix faceting, select the geometry and then from the **Object-Space Modifiers** section of the **Modifier** list, select **Arnold Properties**. In the **Subdivision** rollout, select the **Enable** check box and change **Iterations** to **2**. Also, in the **UV Smoothing** group, select the **Smooth Tangents** check box. Refer to right image in Fig. 11 and the **anisotropic-faceting.max** file.*

The **Rotation** parameter changes the orientation of the anisotropy in the UV space. At **0**, there is not rotation, while at **1** the anisotropy effect is rotated by **180** degrees. The images in Fig. 28 show the output with **Rotation** set to **0.3, 0.7,** and **0.9**. Refer to the **anisotropic-rotation.max** file.

The **Transmission Weight** parameter allows light to scatter through the surface for refractive materials such as glass or water. The images in Fig. 29 show the output with **Transmission Weight** set to **0, 0.5**, and **1**. Refer to the **trans-weight.max** file.

Note: Refraction and the Skydome light

*The **Skydome** light has some limitation when rendering refractive surfaces. In the **trans-weight.max** file, I have used the HDR image in the **Environment Map** slot of the **Environment and Effects** window. You need to adjust the **Global Exposure** value accordingly.*

Caution: Refraction > Ray Depth

*If you see the black color where there should be transparency in the render then you may need to increase the **Transmission > Ray Depth** value in the **Render Setup** window > **Sampling and Ray Depth** rollout.*

The **Transmission Color** parameter controls the transmission color. The longer the light travels inside a medium, the more it gets affected by the transmission color. In other words, the red glass appears dark red as light travels through thicker parts. It is recommended that you use low saturation colors with this parameter.

Caution: Transmission Color

*The **Transmission Color** parameter will only work for the single-sided geometries, if the **Thin-Walled** check box is selected in the **General** group.*

The **Depth** parameter controls the absorption and scattering of the rays. The higher the value you specify for this parameter, the less the light absorption and scattering will be. The images in Fig. 30 show the output with **Transmission Color** set to red and **Depth** set to **0, 3**, and **7**. Refer to the **trans-depth.max** file.

Caution: The Depth parameter
*The **Depth** parameter is scene scale dependent. The transmittance and absorption will depend on the scale of the object. For smaller objects, you need to set a quite a low value for the **Depth** parameter. If you cannot see anything, you may need to check the size of your scene.*

The **Thin-Walled** parameter allows you to simulate translucency effect on single sided geometries. You get the effect of a translucent object being lit from behind. This parameter is ideal for thin-sided object such as bubbles. If you use this parameter with thick objects, the thickness may render incorrectly. The images in Fig. 31 show the output with **Thin-Walled** disabled and enabled. Refer to the **trans-thin-walled.max**.

You can also use the **Thin-Walled** parameter to create effect of light passing through the back of the sheet of a paper. To create this effect, change **Transmission Weight** to **0**, select the **Thin-Walled** check box and then in the **Subsurface** rollout, specify a value for the **Subsurface Weight** parameter.

The images in Fig. 32 show the output with **Subsurface Weight** set to **0, 0.5**, and **1**. Refer to **trans-paper.max**.

The **Exit to Background** parameter traces a ray against the background/environment when the maximum GI reflection/refraction depth is met. Then, it returns the color that is visible in the ray direction. When the parameter is disabled, the ray path is terminated and returns black color on termination of the path. The images in Fig. 33 show the output with **Exit to Background** disabled and enabled. Refer to the **trans-exit-bg.max** file. In this file, a value of **3** is used for **Transmission > Ray Depth**.

Advanced Group

You can create blurry reflections/refractions using the specular **Roughness** parameter [see left image in Fig. 34]. However, if you want to create blurry refraction with the clear reflections, you can use the **Extra Roughness** parameter. It allows you to add some additional blurriness to refraction [see right image in Fig. 34].

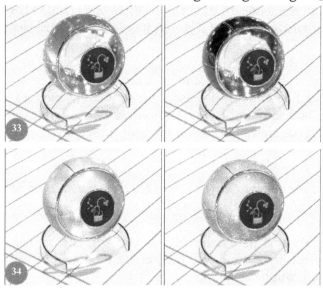

This parameter ranges from **0** [no roughness] to **1**. Refer to **trans-er.max**. In this file, values of **0.05** and **0.3** are used for the specular **Roughness** and **Extra Roughness** parameters, respectively. For the left image, a value of **0.25** is used for the **Roughness** parameter.

The **Dispersion Abbe** parameter defines the **Abbe** number of the material. The **Abbe** number defines how much the **IOR** varies across wavelength. This parameter is especially useful for gemstones such as diamond.

If the **Transmit AOVs** check box is selected, transmission will pass though the AOVs. In this case, if the background is transparent, the transmissive surface becomes transparent and then you can composite the render over another background.

Scatter Group

The scatter **Color** parameter allows you model surface of any liquid that is thick such as honey or a deep body of water. You can also use it to create materials like ice, or milky glass [see Fig. 35]. The **Anisotropy** parameter controls the directional bias of the scattering. Positive values bias the effect forwards [in the direction of the light] whereas negative values backward [towards the light]. Refer to file **trans-scatter.max**.

Subsurface Parameters

Sub-Surface Scattering or SSS allows you to simulate the effect of the light entering an object and scattering beneath its surface. When you enable SSS, not all light gets reflected from the surface, some of it penetrates below the surface of the illuminated object.

Then, some of the scattered light come back out of the surface and becomes visible to the camera. The SSS effect is necessary for simulating surfaces like marble, skin, leaves, was, milk, and so on. SSS is also important when replicating materials such as plastics. Arnold calculates SSS using the brute-force raytracing method.

Caution: Normals
Make sure the normals are facing in the correct direction, otherwise, you will get undesired results.

The **Subsurface Weight** parameter blends between the diffuse and sub-surface scattering. If you specify a value of **0** for weight, there will be only lambert. If you set value to **1**, there will be only SSS.

In most cases, you will use a value of **1** [full SSS]. The **Subsurface Color** parameter defines the color that determines the effect of sub-surface scattering. The images in Fig. 36 show the output with **Subsurface Weight** is set to **0, 0.5**, and **1**. Refer to the **sss-weight.max** file. The images in Fig. 37 show the output when **Subsurface Color** set to red, green, and blue.

The **Scale** parameter controls the distance that light travels under the surface before reflecting back. This parameter is multiplier that multiplies the SSS radius color. The images in Fig. 38 show the output with **Scale** set to **0.5, 1**, and **2**. Refer to **sss-scale.max**.

Caution: The Scale parameter

*The **Scale** parameter is very scale dependent. You need to adjust the value of the scale parameter according to the size of the model.*

The **Radius** parameter controls the distance upto which the light can scatter below the surface. The higher the value you specify for the **Radius** parameter, the smoother the appearance of the scattering effect will be. The lighter the **Subsurface Color**, the more the light will be scattered. A value of **0** produces no scattering effect. The images in Fig. 39 show the output with **Radius** set to **0.25, 0.5,** and **1**. Refer to **sss-radius.max**.

There are two methods available for tracing: **diffusion** and **randomwalk**. You can select one of the methods from the **Type** drop-down list. The **diffusion** method is the default method. Unlike the **diffusion** method, the **randomwalk** method actually traces below the surface with a real random walk and makes no assumptions about the geometry being locally flat. It takes into account the anisotropic scattering like the brute-force volume rendering and produces much better results around concavities and small details. The images in Fig. 40 show the output with **Type** set to **diffusion** and **randomwalk**. Refer to file **sss-type.max**.

The **Anisotropy** parameter defines the **Henyey-Greenstein** anisotropy coefficient between -1 to 1. The default value is **0** which scatters light evenly in all directions.

Positive values bias the scattering effect forwards [in the direction of the light] while negative values bias the scattering backward [toward the light]. The images in Fig. 41 show the output with **Anisotropy** set to **-0.7, 0,** and **0.7**.

 Caution: The Anisotropy parameter
*Note that this parameter only works with the **randomwalk** method.*

Emission Parameters

The options in the **Emission** rollout are used to give the appearance that the material is emitting incandescent light. Note that a **Mesh** light work better in a situation where you need an object to cast realistic looking ray-traced shadows. The **Emission Weight** parameter controls the amount of emitted light. The **Emission Color** parameter defines the emitted color.

Coat Parameters

Clearcoat Group

The **Coat Weight** parameter controls weight of the coat layer. The coat layer simulates a dielectric material which absorbs light and therefore tints all the transmitted light. The **Coat Color** parameter controls the color of the coating layer's transparency. In most of the cases, the **Coat Color** parameter should be set to white. However, you can use it for artistic control.

The left image in Fig. 42 shows material with specular **Roughness** set to **0.4**. The image in the right shows the blue **Coat Color** acts as a clear coat layer with the **Roughness** value of **0.1**, tinting the specular reflection underneath. Refer to **coat-color.max**.

The images in Fig. 43 show the output with **Coat Weight** set to **0, 0.5,** and **1** [Coat Color: RGB **0.937, 0.329, 0**]. A value of **5** was used for the specular **IOR** parameter.

Caution: Coat Layer and Fresnel
*When a low roughness coat is combined on the top of high roughness specular component, the sharp coat will disappear at the center due to **Fresnel**.*

The **Roughness** parameter defines the glossiness of the specular reflections. The lower the value, the sharper the reflections. You can connect a map this parameter to get variations in the coat highlight. The images in Fig. 44 show the output with **Roughness** set to **0.1, 0.5**, and **1**.

The **Coat Normal** parameter controls the Fresnel blending of the coat over the base. You can also use this parameter to create a bumpy coat layer over a smoother base.

For example, you can create a rain effect, flakes on the car paint, or carbon fiber shader. You can also use it to create oily, wet surfaces.

Fig. 45 shows the output when a **Cellular** map is used with the **Coat Normal (Bump)** parameter. Refer to **coat-normal.max**.

The **IOR** parameter controls the fresnel reflectivity of the material. The images in Fig. 30 show the output with **IOR** set to **3, 5**, and **7**. Notice in Fig. 46 that IOR defines the balance between reflections on surfaces facing the viewer and on surface edges, the reflection intensity on the front side changes a lot. Refer to **coat-ior.max**.

Affect Underlying Group

The parameters in this group allow you to create effects like varnished wood. In the real-world, when a material is coated, there is a certain amount of internal reflections on the inside of the coating. As a result, light bounces onto the surface multiple times before escaping and enhances the color of the material. The right image in Fig. 47 shows the result with the underlying **Color** set to **0** and **1**.

The **Roughness** parameter causes the roughness of the coating to have an effect on the roughness of the underlaying layer. As a result, a blurring effect is created that is seen through the top layer.

Sheen Parameters

The parameters in the **Sheen** rollout allow you to create an energy-conserving sheen layer that can use used to simulate micro-fiber and cloth like surfaces such as velvet and satin. You can also use it for leaves, fruits, and for the peach fuzz on the face.

The sheen layer is layer onto the diffuse component and its weight is defined by the **Sheen Weight** parameter. The images in Fig. 48 show the output with **Sheen Weight** set to **0**, **0.1**, and **0.25**. Refer to **sheen-weight.max**.

The **Sheen Color** parameter tints the color of the sheen contribution whereas the **Roughness** parameter controls how much the micro-fibers diverge from the surface normal direction. The images in Fig. 49 show the output with **Sheen Color** set to **[1, 0.918, 0]**, **[1, 0.235, 0]** and **[1, 1, 1]**. The **[0, 0.134, 0.417]** color was used as **Base Color**. Refer to **sheen-color.max**. The images in Fig. 50 show the output with **Roughness** set to **0.1, 0.3**, and **0.6**. Refer to **sheen-roughness.max**.

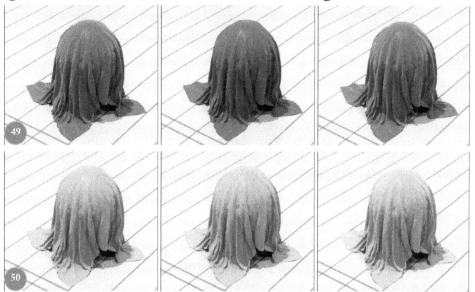

Thin Film Parameters

The parameters in this rollout are used to simulate effect of a thin film interface on a surface. You can use it to create effects like multi-tone car paint, burnt chrome, film on the bubbles, reflective coating on a beetle, and so on.

The **Thickness** parameter controls the actual thickness of the film between the specified min **[0]** and max **[2000]** thickness. The thin film layer affects the specular, transmission, and coat layers. The images in Fig. 51 show the output with **Thickness** set to **300, 400**, and **550**. Refer to **tfilm-thicness.max**.

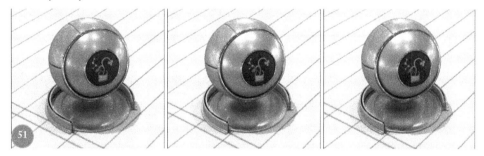

The **IOR** parameter defines the refractive index of the medium surrounding the material. Normally, you want to set it to **1** for air. The images in Fig. 52 show the output with **IOR** set to **1.5, 2**, and **3**. Refer to **tfilm-ior.max**.

Special Features Parameters

The **Opacity (Cutout)** parameter controls the degree to which light is not allowed to travel through it. This parameter affects the whole shader. You can use this parameter to retaining the shadow definition of an object, while making the object itself invisible to the camera. You can connect a normal map usually exported from Mudbox or ZBrush to the **Normal (Bump)** parameter. If the tangent map is available [on which the normal map relies] and exported from your sculpting tool, you can connect it to the **Tangents** parameter.

Two Sided Shader

The **Two Sided** shader applies two shader on either side of a double-sided surface. The **Back** and **Front** parameters are used to input shader for the back and front surfaces, respectively [see Fig. 53].

Volume Shader

Standard Volume

The **Standard Volume** shader is physically-based volume shader. Using this shader, you can independently control volume density, scatter color, and transparent color. The blackbody emission is used to render fire and explosions directly from physics simulations.

 Caution: Rendering
In volume rendering, the shader network is called many times per ray. Therefore, it is recommended to keep the volume shading network as lean as possible.

To use the **Standard Volume** shader, you need a volumetric model. To do so, in the **Create** panel, click **Geometry**, and then select **Arnold** from the drop-down list. Now, in the **Object Type** rollout, click **Volume**, and then drag in the viewport to create the **Volume** object.

Now, in the **Modify** panel, assign the volumetric file path using the **VDB File Path** parameter; the **Select VDB Grids to use** dialog box will be displayed. Select the grids as per your requirements. In this dialog box, if you select the **Set up a default Standard Volume shader** check box, the **Standard Volume** shader will be automatically assigned to the volumetric model. If you don't select this check box, you need to manually assign the shader to the volumetric model. Now, click **OK** to accept the changes.

> *Note: Volumetric models courtesy*
> *The volumetric models used in this book are downloaded from **OpenVDB's** website: **http://www.openvdb.org/download**.*

The **Density** parameter in the **Density** rollout, defines the density of the volume. Higher values generate thick volumes. This parameter acts as a multiplier on the density channel. If no density channel is available, you can connect a shader like the volume sample or a procedural texture. The images in Fig. 54 show the result with **Density** set to **0.1**, **0.25**, and **1**. Also, refer to **volume-density.max**. The **Density Channel** parameter allows to read the density channel from the volume object.

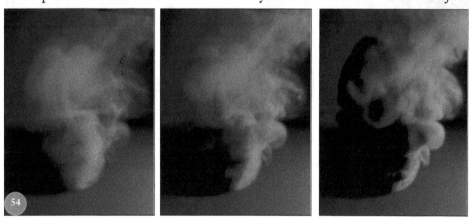

The **Scatter** parameter in the **Scattering** rollout defines the brightness of the volume under illumination. This value is the ratio of the light scattered [not absorbed]. You need to use a value from the range **0** to **1** for energy conservation.

The **Scatter Color** parameter controls the color of the volume under illumination. The **Channel** parameter read the scatter channel from the volume object. It is a multiplier on **Scatter Color**. The images in Fig. 55 show the result with **Scatter Color** set to three different colors: RGB [**0.969, 0.635, 0.455**], RGB[**0.169, 0.11, 0.122**], and RGB [**0.072, 0.068, 0.069**]. Also, refer to **volume-scatter-color.max**.

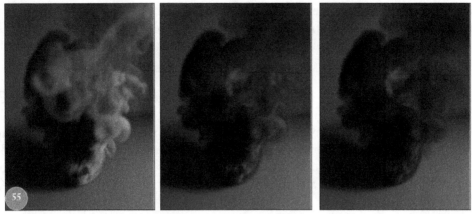

The **Anisotropy** parameter controls the directional bias, or anisotropy of the scattering effect. The default value of **0** scatters light evenly in all directions. It is recommended that you don't use values above **0.95** and below **-0.95** because these value will produce scattering that is so directional that it will not be visible from most of the angles.

The images in Fig. 56 show the result with **Anisotropy** set to **-0.78, 0,** and **0.78**. Also, refer to **volume-density.max**.

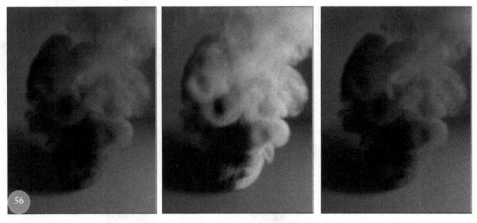

The **Transparency** parameter in the **Transparency** rollout is an additional control for altering density of the volume. It is used to tint the color of the volume shadows and objects seen through the volume.

The **Depth** parameter defines the depth into the volume at which the transparent color is realized. The **Channel** parameter read the transparency channel from the volume object. It is multiplier on **Transparency**.

The images in Fig. 57 show the result with **Transparency** set to three different colors: RGB [**1, 0.3, 0.1**], RGB[**0.8, 0.9, 1**], and RGB [**0.898, 0.914, 0.914**]. A value of **0.3** was used for the **Depth** parameter. Also, refer to **volume-transparency-color.max**.

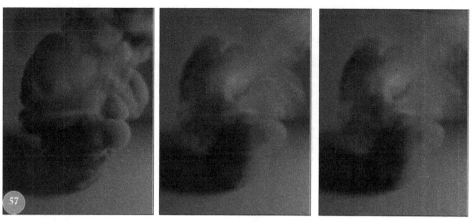

The parameters in the **Emission** rollout are used to control the emission of light. The emission algorithm you can select from the **Mode** drop-down list. Given below is a quick summary:

- **None:** No light is emitted.
- **Channel:** Emits light using a specified emission channel.
- **Density:** Emits light using the density channel.
- **Blackbody:** Emits color and intensity based on temperature, for rendering fire and explosions.

The images in Fig. 58 show the result when **Mode** is set to **None, Channel** [the **heat** channel was used], **Density**, and **Blackbody**. Also, refer to **emission-volume.max**.

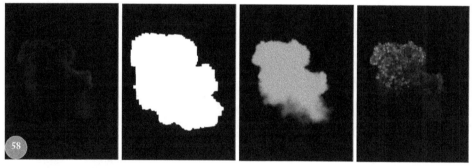

The **Emission** parameter defines the rate at which a volume emits light. If a density, blackbody, or emission channel is used for emission, this parameter acts as a multiplier to decrease or increase the emission. If no such channel is used, you can use a shader like volume sample or procedural texture and connect it to this parameter to control where light is emitted. The **Emission Color** parameter is used to tint the emission.

The **Temperature** parameter in the **Blackbody** rollout is used as a multiplier for the blackbody temperature. Alternatively, you can use a shader like volume sample or procedural texture and connect it to this parameter to control the temperature of the blackbody. The images in Fig. 59 show the result with **Temperature** set to **0.5**, **0.78**, and **1**.

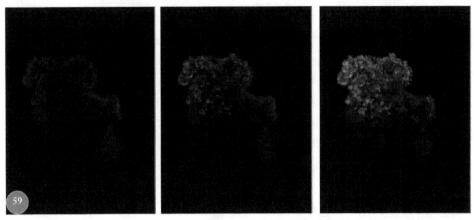

The **Channel** parameter is used to read the temperature channel. The **Kelvin** parameter is used as a multiplier for the temperature. The **Blackbody Intensity** parameter controls the intensity of the blackbody emission.

Utility Shaders

Map to Material Shader

The **Map to Material** shader can be used to assign the map shaders [**Curvature** map, **Utility** map, and so on] that you cannot apply directly to the objects in the scene. Refer to Fig. 60 and **map-to-material.max**. Fig. 60 shows the output of the **Curvature** map using the **Map to Material** shader.

Passthrough Shader

The **Passthrough** shader has **20** inputs **Eval1** to **Eval20** and **Passthrough**. When a shading network is connected to the **Passthrough** shader, the shader connected to the **Passthrough** port is evaluated first and passed as-is to output. This shader is used with AOVs. See **Unit A6 > Exercise 2** for more details about how to define a custom AOV in the scene.

Ray Switch Shader

Ray Switch Shader is used to evaluate different shader trees per ray. This feature gives you more artistic control. You can control the camera, shadow, diffuse reflection, diffuse transmission, specular reflection, specular transmission, and volume rays using this shader. For example, if you want to give different appearance to an area which is behind a glass object, connect an input shader to the **Specular Transmission** parameter of the **Ray Switch** shader [see Fig. 61]. Also, refer to **ray-switch-shader.max**.

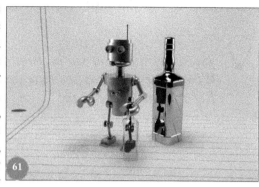

Switch Shader

Switch Shader is used to switch between different shader. There are **20** ports [**input0** to **input19**] available on the **Switch Shader** node. You can make a shader active by entering its index number in the **Index** field. For example, if you want to make **input2** active, enter **1** in the **Index** field. Refer to **switch-shader.max**.

Trace Set

You can use the **Trace Set** shader to tag the rays so that it hit or avoid tagged objects. This feature may be removed in a future version of Arnold.

AOV Shaders

The AOV Shaders allows you to write float, int or color data to custom AOVs. You can use these nodes to create custom AOVs. See **Unit A6 > Exercise 1** for more details about how to define a custom AOV in the scene.

Subdivisions and Displacement Mapping

The displacement and subdivision mapping settings can be accessed via the **Arnold Properties** modifier [see Fig. 62]. Each rollout has one or more **Enable** checkboxes [see Fig. 63] that you can use to override the defaults on just the part you want to control. If you collapse the stack the modifier will remain.

Subdivision

Before we discuss the displacement mapping, lets first have a look at subdivision settings. Select the **Enable** check box in the **Subdivision** rollout to enable subdivision settings. The options in the **Type** drop-down list allow you select the subdivision algorithm. The **None** option renders the mesh as is. The **Linear** option adds vertices at the center of the each face. The **Catmull-Clark** option creates smooth surface using quadrilateral faces. The images in Fig. 64 show the result with **Type** set to **None, Linear,** and **Catmull-Clark**. Refer to **subd-type.max**.

Tip: Wireframe render
The wireframe you see in Fig. 40 is created by connecting the Arnold's **Wireframe** *utility to the* **base_color** *port of the* **Standard Surface** *shader. Refer to* **subd-type.max**.

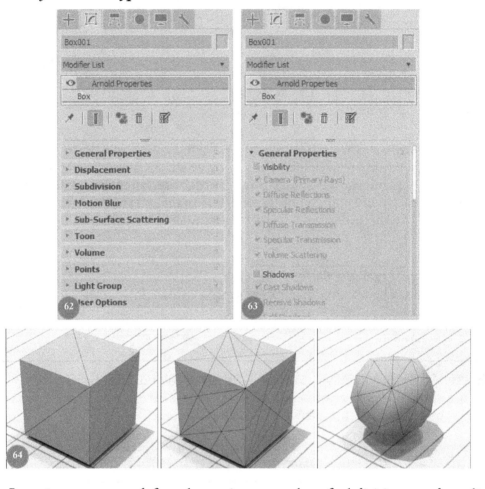

The **Iterations** parameter defines the maximum number of subdivision rounds applied to the mesh. The images in Fig. 65 show the result with **Type** set to **Catmull-Clark** and **Iterations** set to **1, 2,** and **3**.

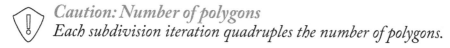 **Caution: Number of polygons**
Each subdivision iteration quadruples the number of polygons.

The **Metric** parameter controls the amount of error between a given subdivision level and the limit surface.

- **Flatness:** You can use it when the curvature of the mesh in pixels is the feature used to choose the adaptive subdivision level.
- **Edge Length:** When the length of the polygonal edges in pixels is used.
- **Automatic:** This option uses **Flatness** when no displacement is applied. It uses **Edge Length** when a displacement map is applied to the mesh.

The **Error** parameter defines the maximum allowable difference in pixels between the adoptively chosen subdivision level and the "limit" subdivided surface. The options in the **Space** drop-down allow you to define the subdivision space. The adaptive subdivision in the raster space does not work well when the **Raster** space is used. Using the **Object** space ensures that all instances will subdivide properly.

The parameters in **UV Smoothing** group are useful for anisotropic shaders to get distortion free anisotropic highlights. If you notice faceting in the anisotropic highlights, use the **Smooth Tangents** check box.

 Caution: The Smooth Tangents parameter and memory consumption
*When you use **Smooth Tangents**, there will be memory overhead [approx. **100** extra bytes per vertex per keyframe].*

Displacement

Unlike bump maps, the displacement maps alter the geometry. As a result, correct silhouette, and self-shadowing effects are generated. You can use it to add the surface details that would take lots of time using the regular modeling methods. The displacement mapping occurs in two ways:

- The Float, RGB & RGBA inputs displace geometry along the normal.
- The vector input displaces geometry along the vector.

 Caution: Number of polygons
Make sure that your base geometry have sufficient numbers of polygons in order to get the predictable results. Also, ensure that you use highest quality texture maps for the displacement mapping.

 Tip: .tx files
*Arnold works well with high resolution maps as long as you process the maps using the **maketx** utility. This utility convert textures to **.tx** files. The **.tx** files are mipmapped tiles files.*

Note: The maketx utility
*This utility was developed by Larry Gritz at Sony Pictures Imageworks. For more info, visit: **http://www.openimageio.org**.*
Usage:
maketx [options] file...
eg: maketx -v -u --oiio --checknan --filter lanczos3 path/to/fileIn.tif -o path/to/fileOut.tx

*You can find this plugin at the following location: **C:\ProgramData\Autodesk\ApplicationPlugins\MAXtoA**.*

In Arnold, displacement settings affect object on a per-object basis. It is useful when you want to use the same map for two different results. To enable displacement feature, select the **Enable** check box in the **Displacement** rollout. To use a texture map, select the **Use Map** check box in the **Displacement Map** group and then drag texture from the material editor to the **No Map** button.

The **Height** parameter controls the amount of displacement. You can enter a negative or a positive value for this parameter. This parameter only affects with the normal displacement. The images in Fig. 66 show the result with **Height** set to **0**, **1**, and **5**. Refer to **disp.max**.

The **Zero** parameter defines a floating point value which shifts the displacement map. It defines the value of the displacement map that is considered zero displacement. The **Bounds Pad** parameter is used to extend the bounding box of the mesh to include any additional displacement coming from the shader.

When the **Enable Autobump** check box is selected, Arnold puts the high frequencies of a displacement map into the bump attribute. As a result, you don't need high subdivision iteration value. This check box is selected by default.

Caution: UV Coordinates
The autobump algorithm needs UV coordinates to compute the surface tangents. Therefore, make sure that the mesh has a UV set applied to it.

On changing the subdivision type to **Catmull-Clark** or **Linear** and increasing the iteration value will improve the displacement quality. However, be careful when increasing the value because each iteration quadruples the geometry.

Hands-on Exercises

Exercise 1: Creating the Copper Material

In this exercise, we will create the copper material using the **Standard Surface** material. Fig. E1 shows the rendered output.

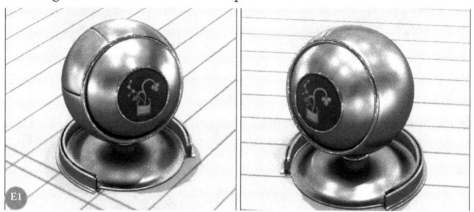

Table E1 summarizes the exercise.

Table E1	
Difficulty level	Intermediate
Estimated time to complete	15 Minutes
Topics in exercise	• Getting Started • Creating the Material
Resources folder	**unit-a3**
Start file	**shader-ball-01.max**
Final exercise file	**copper-material-finish.max**

Getting Started
Open **shader-ball-01.max** in 3ds Max and make sure the **Physical** camera is active.

Creating the Material
Follow these steps:

1. Open **Slate Material Editor** and then double-click on **sample-mat** swatch.

2. In the **Parameter Editor > Base** rollout > **Base Color** group, change **Base Weight** to **1** and **Base Color** to RGB [**0.926, 0.721, 0.504**], see Fig. E2. In the **Specular** rollout > **General** group, change **Specular Color** to RGB [**0.996, 0.957, 0.823**], see Fig. E3.

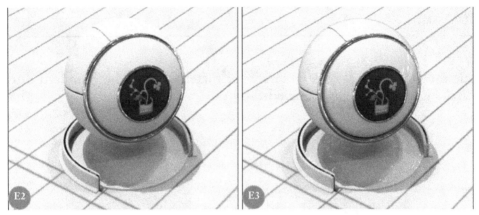

3. In the **Specular** rollout > **Advanced** group, change **Metalness** to **1** [see Fig. E4]. In the **Specular** rollout > **General** group, change **Roughness** to **0.15** [see Fig. E5].

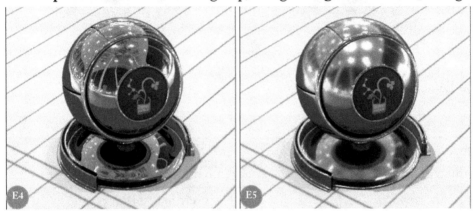

4. In **Slate Material Editor**, double-click on the **sample-mat** node > **specular-roughness** port to open **Material/Map Browser**. Double-click on **Bitmap** in the **Maps** > **General** rollout. In the **Select Bitmap Image File** dialog box, double-click on **dirt-a.png** to select it [see Fig. E6].

5. In the **Parameter Editor** > **dirt-a.png** bitmap > **Output** rollout, select the **Invert** check box followed by the **Enable Color Map** check box. Now, change the color map, as shown in Fig. E7. Fig. E8 shows the render.

6. In **Slate Material Editor**, double-click on the **sample-mat** node > **normal** port to open **Material/Map Browser**. Double-click on **Bump2D** in the **Maps** > **Arnold** > **Bump** rollout.

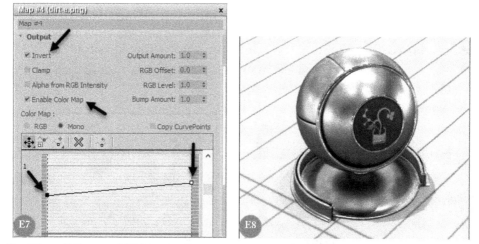

7. In **Slate Material Editor,** connect output of the **dirt-a.png** bitmap with the **bump_map** port of the **Bump 2D** node [see Fig. E9].

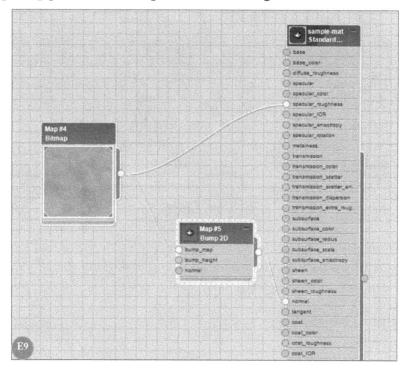

8. In the **Parameter Editor > Bump 2D > Parameters** rollout, change **Bump Height** to **0.05**.

Exercise 2: Creating the Honey Material

In this exercise, we will create the honey material using the transmission component of the **Standard Surface** material. Fig. E1 shows the rendered output.

Table E2 summarizes the exercise.

Table E2	
Difficulty level	Intermediate
Estimated time to complete	30 Minutes
Topics in this exercise	• Getting Started • Creating the Material
Resources folder	**unit-a3**
Start file	**dragon-transmission.max**
Final exercise file	**honey-finish.max**

Getting Started

Open **dragon-transmission.max** in 3ds Max and make sure the **Physical** camera is active.

Creating the Material

Follow these steps:

1. Open **Slate Material Editor** and then double-click on **sample-mat** swatch.

2. In the **Parameter Editor > Base** rollout > **Base Color** group, change **Base Weight** to **0**.

3. In the **Specular** rollout > **Advanced** group, change **IOR** to **1.48**. In the **Transmission** rollout > **General** group, change **Transmission Weight** to **1** and then change **Transmission Color** to RGB [0.647, 0.257, 0.028] and **Depth** to **0.5** [see Fig. E2].

4. In the **Transmission** rollout > **Scatter** group, change **Color** to RGB [0.647, 0.41, 0.27], see Fig. E3. In the **Specular** rollout > **General** group, change **Roughness** to **0.25**.

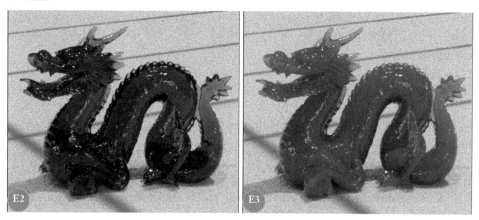

Exercise 3: Creating the Chocolate Material

In this exercise, we will create the chocolate material using the transmission component of the **Standard Surface** material. Fig. E1 shows the rendered output.

Table E3 summarizes the exercise.

Table E3	
Difficulty level	Intermediate
Estimated time to complete	30 Minutes
Topics in this exercise	• Getting Started • Creating the Material
Resources folder	**unit-a3**
Start file	**dragon-transmission.max**
Final exercise file	**chocolate-finish.max**

Getting Started

Open **dragon-transmission.max** in 3ds Max and make sure the **Physical** camera is active.

Creating the Material

Follow these steps:

1. Open **Slate Material Editor** and then double-click on **sample-mat** swatch.

2. In the **Parameter Editor > Base** rollout > **Base Color** group, change **Base Weight** to **0**.

3. In the **Transmission** rollout > **General** group, change **Transmission Weight** to **1** and then change **Transmission Color** to **RGB [2, 0.799, 0.705]** and **Depth** to **0.15** [see Fig. E2].

4. In the **Transmission** rollout > **Scatter** group, change **Color** to **RGB [0.878, 0.208, 0]**, see Fig. E3.

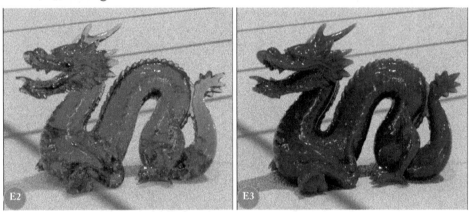

5. In the **Advanced** rollout, change **Extra Roughness** to **0.3**. In the **Specular** rollout > **General** group, change **Roughness** to **0.15**.

Exercise 4: Creating the Car Paint Material

In this exercise, we will create the car paint material using the **Standard Surface** material. Fig. E1 shows the rendered output. Table E4 summarizes the exercise.

Table E4	
Difficulty level	Intermediate
Estimated time to complete	30 Minutes
Topics in this exercise	• Getting Started • Creating the Material
Resources folder	**unit-a3**

Table E4	
Start file	**sss-studio.ma**
Final exercise file	**car-paint-finish.max**

E1

Getting Started

Open **shader-ball-01.max** in 3ds Max and make sure the **Physical** camera is active.

Creating the Material

Follow these steps:

1. Open **Slate Material Editor** and then double-click on **sample-mat** swatch.

2. In the **Parameter Editor > Base** rollout > **Base Color** group, change **Base Weight** to **0.7** and **Base Color** to **RGB [0.044, 0.326, 0.604]**.

3. In the **Specular** rollout > **General** group, change **Specular Weight** to **1** and **Specular Color** to **RGB [0.101, 0.996, 0.079]**. In the **General** group, change **Roughness** to **0.1**. In the **Advanced** group, change **IOR** to **5**, see Fig. E2.

4. In the **Coat** rollout, change **Coat Weight** to **1**. In the **Affect Underlying** group, change **Color** to **0.2**, see Fig. E3.

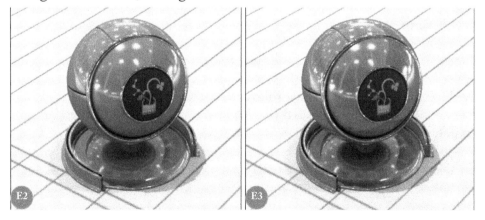

E2

E3

5. In the **Thin Film** rollout, change **Thickness** to **500**.

Exercise 5: Creating the Wax Material

In this exercise, we will create the wax material using the **Standard Surface** material. Fig. E1 shows the rendered output.

Table E5 summarizes the exercise.

Table E5	
Difficulty level	Intermediate
Estimated time to complete	30 Minutes
Topics in this exercise	• Getting Started • Creating the Material
Resources folder	**unit-a3**
Start file	**sss-studio.max**
Final exercise file	**wax-finish.max**

Getting Started
Open **ssss-studio.max** in 3ds Max and make sure the **Physical** camera is active.

Creating the Material
Follow these steps:

1. Open **Slate Material Editor** and then double-click on **sample-mat** swatch.

2. In the **Parameter Editor > Base** rollout > **Base Color** group, change **Base Weight** to **0.7** and **Base Color** to RGB [**0.439, 0.011, 0.422**]. Also, change **Roughness** to **0.4**, see Fig. E2.

3. In the **Specular** rollout > **General** group, change **Roughness** to **0.4**. In the **Specular** rollout > **Advanced** group, change **IOR** to **1.67**, see Fig. E3.

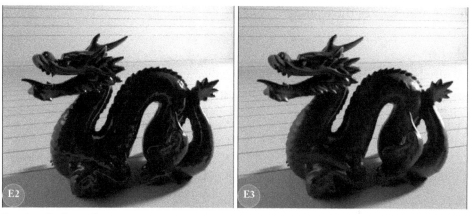

4. In the **Subsurface** rollout, change **Subsurface Weight** to **1**, **Subsurface Color** to RGB [**0.439, 0.174, 0.428**], and **Scale** to **0.7**, see Fig. E4.

5. Change **Radius X, Y,** and **Z** to **0.4** each, see Fig. E5. Change **Type** to **randomwalk**.

Exercise 6: Studio Automotive Rendering

In this exercise, we will render an automobile style shot. Fig. E1 shows the rendered output.

Table E6 summarizes the exercise.

Table E6	
Difficulty level	Advanced
Estimated time to complete	40 Minutes
Topics in the exercise	• Getting Started • Adding Light • Creating Material for the Floor • Creating Material for the Reflector • Creating Material for the Car's Body
Resources folder	**unit-a3**
Start file	**auto-start.max**
Final exercise file	**auto-finish.max**

Getting Started
Open **auto-start.max** in 3ds Max and make sure the **Physical** camera is active.

Adding Light
Follow these steps:

1. In the **Create** panel, click **Lights,** and then select **Arnold** from the drop-down list below **Lights.** Now, in the **Object Type** rollout, click **Arnold Light,** and then change **Type** to **Quad.** Now, click-drag in the **Front** viewport to create a light [see Fig. E2].

2. In the **Modify** panel > **Shape** rollout, change **Quad X** and **Quad Y** to **1.952** and **2.857,** respectively. Now, align the light [see Fig. E3]. Render the scene [see Fig. E4].

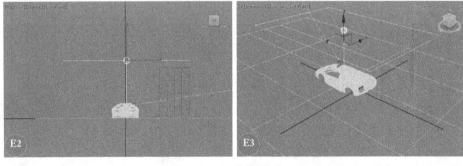

3. Select light in the scene and then in the **Modify** panel > **Color/Intensity** rollout > **Intensity** group, change **Intensity** to **5** and **Exposure** to **10.** In the **Rendering** rollout, change **Samples** to **4.** Render the scene [see Fig. E5].

Creating Material for the Floor

Follow these steps:

1. Open **Slate Material Editor** and then create a **Standard Surface** shader node in the active view. Rename the shader as **mat-floor** and apply it to **floor-geo**. Create a **Ramp Rgb** node from **Maps > Arnold > Texture** rollout to the active view. Connect the **Ramp Rgb** node to the **base_color** port of **mat-floor**.

2. In the **Parameter Editor > mat-floor > Base** rollout, change **Base Color Weight** to **0.3**. In the **Specular** rollout, change **Roughness** to **0.4**. Render the scene [see Fig. E6]. Now, change the ramp for the **Ramp Rgb** node, as shown in Fig. E7.

3. Render the scene [see Fig. E8].

Creating Material for the Reflector

Follow these steps:

1. Open **Slate Material Editor** and then create a **Standard Surface** shader node in the active view. Rename the shader as **mat-ref** and apply it to **ref-plane-geo**.

2. In the **Parameter Editor > mat-ref > Base** rollout, change **Base Color Weight** to **0**. In the **Emission** rollout, change **Emission Weight** to **1**.

Creating Material for the Car's Body
Follow these steps:

1. Add a **Car Paint** shader node to the active view and then rename it as **mat-car-body**. Now, apply it to **car-body**.

2. In the **Base** rollout, change **Base** to **0.2**, **Base Color** to RGB [**0.016, 0.031, 0.216**], and **Base Roughness** to **0.3**. Render the scene [see Fig. E9].

3. In the **Specular** rollout, change **Specular Color** to RGB [**0.216, 0.843, 0.996**], **Specular Roughness** to **0.5**, and **Specular IOR** to **6.0**. Render the scene [see Fig. E10].

What next?
*Now, we will use a **Ramp Rgb** node to modulate the specular reflection from the base coat depending on the viewing angle.*

4. Add a **Ramp Rgb** map node to the active view and connect it to the **specular_flip_flop** port of the **mat-car-body** node. Now, change the ramp, as shown in Fig. 11. Use the following two colors: RGB [**55, 215, 254**] and RGB [**4, 8, 55**]. Render the scene [see Fig. E12].

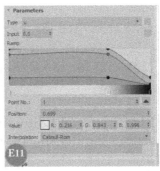

What next?
*Now, we will assign a color to modulate the base coat specular color of the area facing the light source using the **Specular Light Facing** parameter.*

5. In the **mat-car-body > Specular** rollout, change **Specular Light Facing** to RGB [**0.722, 0, 0.957**] and **Specular Falloff** to **0.07**. Render the scene [see Fig. E13].

What next?
Now, we will add flakes to the car paint.

6. Copy the **Specular Color** parameter's color value from the **Specular** rollout and then paste it on the color swatch of **Flake Color** parameter in the **Flakes** rollout.

7. In the active view, connect the **Ramp Rgb** node connected to the **specular_flip_flop** port to the **flake_flip_flop** port. Change **Flake Density** to **0.02** and **Normal Randomize** to **0.2**. Render the scene [see Fig. E14].

What next?
Let's now adjust the intensity of the light.

What just happened?
Notice the blown highlights on the hood of the car in Fig. E14. We can reduce the effect by adjusting the exposure of the light. As a result, the overall illumination of the scene will be reduced, which is what we don't want. We can get the same effect by reducing the specular contribution of the light. Also, we need to reduce weight of the emission of the reflective plane. Let's do it.

8. Select light and then in the **Modify** panel > **Contribution** rollout, change **Specular** to **0.5** and then render the scene [see Fig. E15].

9. In the **mat-ref** shader > **Parameter Editor** > **Emission** rollout, change **Emission Weight** to **0.5**. Render the scene [see Fig. E16].

10. Press **F10** to open the **Render Setup** window. In the **Arnold Renderer** panel > **Sampling and Ray Depth** rollout, change **Camera (AA)**, **Diffuse**, and **Specular** samples to **5**, **6**, and **4** respectively. Also, change **Ray Depth [Diffuse]** to **2**. Render the scene [see Fig. E17].

Quiz

Multiple Choice
Answer the following questions, only one choice is correct.

1. Which of the following materials are supported by Arnold?

   [A] Multi/Sub-Object   [B] Shell
   [C] Arch & Design   [D] All of these

2. Which of the following parameters allow light to scatter through the surface for refractive materials such as glass or water?

   [A] Transmission Weight   [B] Transparency
   [C] Transmission Roughness   [D] None of these

3. Which of the following shader allows you to mix up to eight shaders together?

   [A] Mix   [B] Blend
   [C] Layer   [D] Top Bottom

4. Which of the following layers is not available in the **Car Paint** Shader?

   [A] Base   [B] Specular
   [C] Coat   [D] Base Color

Fill in the Blanks
Fill in the blanks in each of the following statements:

1. When _____ is running, material previews in the material editor are not rendered because only one render session can be active in Arnold.

2. Arnold's _____ shader is energy conversing by default.

3. The _____ parameter defines the base diffuse color of the **Standard Surface** shader.

4. The base component of the **Standard Surface** shader follows the _____ reflection model with surface roughness.

5. The _____ parameter is used to define the fresnel reflectivity of the material.

6. The transmission _____ parameter is scene scale dependent.

7. The _____ effect is necessary for simulating surfaces like marble, skin, leaves, was, and milk.

8. In the SSS layer, the _____ parameter controls the distance upto which the light can scatter below the surface.

9. In SSS layer, there are two methods available for tracing: _____ and _____.

10. The coat layer simulates a _____ material which absorbs light and therefore tints all the transmitted light.

11. The _____ parameter controls the index of refraction of the base coat of the **Car Paint** shader.

12. The _____ parameter in the _____ rollout allows you to tint the specular highlight from flakes.

13. The _____ shader allows you to mix up to eight shaders together.

14. The _____ shader allows you to create holdout effects by rendering alpha as **0**.

15. To resemble the appearance of the human hair, it is recommended that you leave _____ as pure white and use the _____ controls to get the plausible colors.

16. To render hair in 3ds Max, the scene must contain a _____ effect.

True or False
State whether each of the following is true or false:

1. Arnold does not support most of the legacy 3ds Maps.

2. If you use **OSL** maps with the Arnold's **Standard Surface** shader, the texture displayed in the viewport will not match the texture displayed in the rendered output.

3. The **Indirect Diffuse** parameter traces a ray against the background/environment when the maximum GI depth [reflection/refraction] is met and return the color of the background/environment in that direction.

4. The **Thin-Walled** parameter allows you to simulate translucency effect on single sided geometries.

5. The lighter the **Subsurface Color**, the less the light will be scattered.

6. In the SSS layer, the **Anisotropy** parameter works only with the **diffusion** type.

7. When a low roughness coat is combined on the top of high roughness specular component, the sharp coat will disappear at the center due to Fresnel.

8. In the **Thin Film** layer, the **IOR** parameter defines the refractive index of the medium surrounding the material.

9. In the **Car Paint** shader, if you a specify a value of **0** for the **Flake Density** parameter, the surface will be fully covered with flakes.

10. For blond and bright colored hair, a higher number of specular bounces are required to get accurate results.

11. The **Melanin** parameter lets you control the natural hair colors.

12. The **Two Sided** shader applies two shader on either side of a double-sided surface.

13. The **Standard Volume** shader is physically-based volume shader.

14. Each subdivision iteration quadruples the number of polygons.

Summary

In this unit, the following topics are covered:

- Shaders
- Materials
- Subdivision and Displacement mapping
- Legacy 3ds Max maps

Unit A4: Arnold Maps

Arnold supports most of the legacy 3ds Max Maps such as **Gradient, Noise,** and so on using a feature that calls native C++ maps [not materials]. There are many Arnold maps that you can use with the Arnold materials and shaders. These maps are categorized in different groups, namely **Bump, Color, Conversion, Environment, Math, Shading State, Surface, Texture, User Data, Utility, Volume,** and **Cryptomatte.** In this unit, we will discuss various Arnold maps.

Bump Maps

Bump 2D

The **Bump 2D** map allows you to create bump mapping based on a 2D texture map. Unlike the displacement mapping, bump mapping doesn't alter the shape of the geometry. Make sure that UV coordinates are available with the geometry in order to drive perturbation. The **Bump Height** parameter is used to scale the height of the bump map output. The right image in Fig. 1 shows the result of the bump mapping. The **Noise** map used as bump in this example, is shown in the left image in Fig. 1. Fig. 2 shows the **Noise** map connected to the **Bump 2D** map which is connected to the **Normal** port of the **Standard Surface** shader. Also, refer to **bump2d-map.max.**

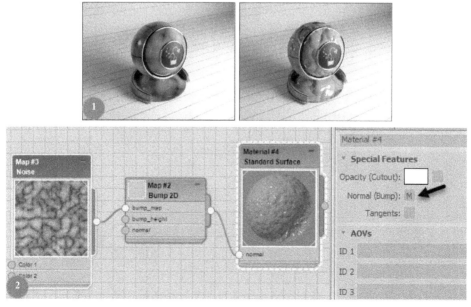

Bump 3D

The **Bump 3D** map is used to provide bump map based on a 3D input. In 3D bump mapping, the bump input is calculated at different points. The right image in Fig. 3 shows the result of the 3D bump mapping. The **Noise** map used as bump in this example, is shown in the left image. Fig. 4 shows the **Noise** map connected to the **Bump 3D** map which is connected to the **Normal** port of the **Standard Surface** shader. Also, refer to **bump2d-map.max**.

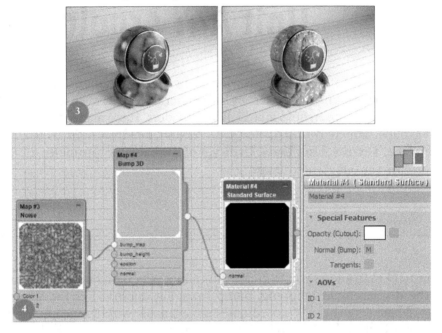

> **Caution: File textures**
> *If you are using file images as textures, you should use the **Bump 2D** map.*

Normal Map

Normal Map is used to replace the interpolated surface normal by the one evaluated from a RGB texture. Each RGB channel in the texture corresponds to the X, Y, and Z coordinates of the surface normal. You need to connect texture to the **Input** parameter.

The first two images in Fig. 5 show the output with and without **Normal Map**. The third image shows the normal map used. Fig. 6 shows the node network. Also, refer to **normal-map.max**.

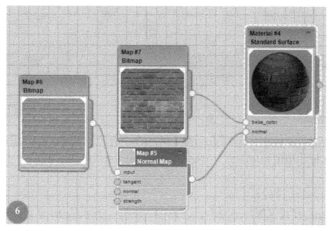

Round Corners

The **Round Corners** map allows you to give appearance of a round corner near the edges by modifying the shading normals. This shader is particularly useful on those hard surface models where you have not modeled beveled edges thus saving a lot of time. You can connect this shader to the **Normal** or **Coat Normal** parameter of the **Standard Surface** shader. Refer to **round-corners-map.max**.

> *Caution: Normals*
> *This map will not work correctly if the normals are not correctly oriented on the object.*

> *Tip: Multiple bump maps*
> *You can use the **normal** input port of the **Round Corners** map to chain multiple bump maps.*

> *Tip: Displacement*
> *The **Round Corners** map also works with displacement.*

The **Samples** parameter allows you to define the number of raytracing samples used to compute the round normal. You can remove the round noise artifacts by increasing the value of this parameter. The images in Fig. 7 show the output with **Samples** set to **0, 6**, and **9**.

The **Radius** parameter controls the radius of the edge fillet. The higher the value you specify, the wider the rounding effect will be. The images in Fig. 8 show the output with **Radius** set to **0, 0.1**, and **2**.

If you specify a normal using the **Normal** parameter, it will be used for the roundness. If empty, the underlying surface normals will be used.

Tip: Normal AOV
*The normal AOV [N] can be used to check how the **Round Corners** map rounds the shading normals, see Fig. 9. Also, refer to **round-corners-map-n.max**.*

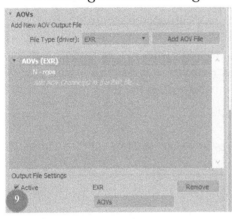 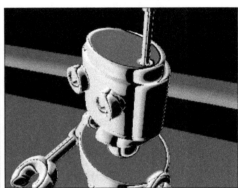

Color Maps

Color Convert
The **Color Convert** map allows you to convert an input color to RGB color space, to HSV color space, and vice-versa.

Color Correct
The **Color Correct** map is used to adjust the gamma, hue, saturation, contrast, and exposure of an input image. The **Gamma** parameter applies a gamma correction to the color. The images in Fig. 10 show the output with **Gamma** set to **1**, **2**, and **3**. Also, refer to **color-correct.max**.

The **Hue Shift** parameter allows you to rotate the color hue. A value of **1** means a full rotation. The images in Fig. 11 show the output with **Hue Shift** set to **0.3, 0.4,** and **0.8.**

The **Saturation** parameter is used to scale the saturation of the image. The images in Fig. 12 show the output with **Saturation** set to **0, 1,** and **2.**

The **Contrast** parameter scales the contrast values around the contrast pivot. The images in Fig. 13 show the output with **Contrast** set to **0.1, 0.5,** and **0.8.** The contrast pivot can be controlled using the **Contrast Pivot** parameter.

The **Exposure** value multiplies color using a f-stop value. An increment of **1** will double the luminosity. The images in Fig. 14 show the output with **Exposure** set to **0, 1,** and **2.**

The value of the **Multiply** parameter is multiplied to the color value. The middle image in Fig. 15 shows the output when yellow color is multiplied with the input color [see the left image].

The value of the **Add** parameter is added to the input color value. The right-most image in Fig. 15 shows the output when yellow color is added with the input color. Also, refer to **color-correct-add.max**. The **Mask** parameter is used to blend between the input color and the color-corrected one.

In the output shown in Fig. 16, I have masked the color using the **Noise** map. The result shown in the right-most image of Fig. 15, yellow color was used as the **Input** color. Refer to **color-correct-mask.max**.

Color Jitter

The **Color Jitter** map allows you to alter the input color by applying a random color variation. You can specify random values for the hue, saturation, and gain components. The **Obj. Seed** setting is used to get a different random variation.

The **Input** parameter in the **Input** rollout defines the base color for the **Color Jitter** map. The **Obj. Gain Min/Max** parameters in the **Object** rollout defines the range of the random value to be added to the gain. The random value is generated based on the name of the object.

The images in Fig. 17 show the output with **Obj. Gain Min/Max** set to **0/-1, 0/0,** and **0/1**. The values of the **Input Color** and **Obj. Hue Min** parameters were set to RGB **[1, 1, 1]** and **0.5**, respectively. Also, refer to **color-jitter.max**.

The **Obj. Hue Min/Max** and **Obj. Saturation Min/Max** parameters are used to define the range of a random value added to the hue and saturation, respectively.

The images in Fig. 18 show the output with **Obj. Hue Min/Max** set to **0/0, 0/1,** and **-0.5/0.5**. Also, refer to **color-jitter-hue.max**. The **Obj. Seed** parameter generates a different color variation.

Likewise, the parameters in the **Face, User Data,** and **Procedural** rollouts are used to generate color variations based on the primitive id, the data_input, and the procedural object, respectively.

Conversion Maps

Float to Int
The **Float to Int** map converts float to an integer value.

Float to Matrix
The **Float to Matrix** map constructs a 4x4 matrix from float values for each element.

Float to RGB
The **Float to RGB** map creates RGB color from individual R, G, and B float values.

Float to RGBA
The **Float to RGBA** map creates RGBA color from R, G, B, and A float values.

RGB to Float
The **RGB to Float** map converts RGB color to float value.

RGB to Vector
The **RGB to Vector** map converts RGB color to vector.

RGBA to Float
The **RGBA to Float** map converts RGB color and alpha values to float.

Shuffle
The **Shuffle** map combines RGB and alpha inputs to output an RGBA. Additionally, you can shuffle channels, you can choose which of R, G, B, and A input channels go to which R, G, B, and A output channels.

Vector Map
In the conventional displacement mapping, surface is only displaced in a direction perpendicular to the polygon of base mesh. Vector displacement maps can be displaced in directions other than the face normals. **Vector Map** allows you to displace a surface in multiple directions using the tangent space vector.

Vector to RGB

The **Vector to RGB** map converts vector to RGB color. Also, refer to **state-vector.max**.

Math Maps

Abs

The **Abs** map return the absolute value of the **Input** parameter.

Add

The **Add** map returns the sum of the **Input 1** and **Input 2** parameters.

Atan

The **Atan** map returns the arctangent of input **Y**/ input **X**.

Compare

The **Compare** map compares the values of **Input 1** and **Input 2** with the following **Test** operators and returns true or false:

- Equal (==)
- Not Equal (!=)
- Greater Than (>)
- Less Than (<)
- Greater Than or Equal (>=)
- Less Than or Equal (<=)

Complement

The **Complement** map returns the following value: (**1 - Input**). You can use this map to invert an image. Refer to **complement.max**.

Cross

The **Cross** map computes the cross product between two vectors: **Input 1** and **Input 2**.

Divide

The **Divide** map returns the following value: (**Input 1/Input 2**).

Dot

The **Dot** map computes the dot product between two vectors: **Input 1** and **Input 2**.

Exp

The **Exp** map returns the following value: e^{Input}.

Fraction

The **Fraction** map returns the fractional part of the **Input** parameter. For example, an input of **456.293** would return **0.293**.

Is Finite

The **Is Finite** map returns false if **Input** is either infinity or **NaN**, and true otherwise.

Length

The **Length** map returns the length of the **Input** vector.

Log

The **Log** map returns logarithm of **Input** to base **Base**. This is the inverse of **Pow**.

Matrix Multiply Vector

The **Matrix Multiply Vector** map is used to multiply a vector by a matrix [for example, a matrix generated by **matrix_transform**].

Matrix Transform

The **Matrix Transform** map is used to create a matrix using the rotation, translation, scale, and pivot settings.

Max

The **Max** map returns the per-component maximum of **Input 1** and **Input 2**.

Min

The **Min** map returns the per-component minimum of **Input 1** and **Input 2**.

Mix RGBA

The **Mix RGBA** map is used to blend two colors or textures. This map outputs a linear interpolation of the two inputs according to the **Mix** parameter. The right-most image in Fig. 19 shows the mix output of the textures, shown in the left and middle images of Fig. 19. A **Mix** weight value of **0.4** was used for mixing.

Modulo

The **Modulo** map returns **Input** modulo **Divisor**. The result is the remainder of the division of **Input** by **Divisor**.

Multiply

The **Multiply** map returns the following value: **Input 1 * Input 2**. Refer to **multiply.max**.

Negate

The **Negate** map returns -input [-**The input color to be negated**].

Normalize

The **Normalize** map returns a normalized **Input** vector [a unit vector pointing in the same direction].

Pow

The **Pow** map returns **Base**^{Exponent}. The resulting value is the inverse of **Log**.

Random

The **Random** map is used to output a random color from various types of inputs. Refer to **random.max**.

Range

The **Range** map is used to linearly remap the **Input** shader from input range [**Input Min .. Input Max**] to the output range [**Output Min .. Output Max**]. If the **Smoothstep** check box is selected, remapping is done using a smooth step function. Otherwise, its done linearly. Refer to **range.max**.

Reciprocal

The **Reciprocal** map returns the multiplicative inverse of **Input: 1/Input** or **Input-1**.

Sign

The **Sign** map returns **-1** if **Input < 0, 0** if **Input == 0**, and **1** if **Input > 0**.

Space Transform

The **Space Transform** map converts the **Input** coordinates from one space to another: **World, Object, Camera, Screen**, and **Tangent**.

Sqrt

The **Sqrt** map returns square root of **Input**.

Subtract

The **Subtract** map returns the following value: **Input 1 - Input 2**.

Trigo

The **Trigo** map is used to perform various trigonometric functions on **Input: cos, sin, tan, acos, asin, atan, cosh, sinh**, and **tanh**.

Shading State Maps

The **Shading State** maps allow you to access the ray and geometry properties such as ray origin, ray direction, shading normals, and so on.

State Vector

You can use the **State Vector** map to output shading normals, including smooth normals, and bump maps as vectors. Refer to **state-vector.max**. The images in Fig. 20 show the result when **Variable** is set to **Rd** and **N**.

State Int

The **State Int** map is used to output variables such as bounces, ray type, number of active lights, and so on as integer values.

State Float

The **State Float** map is used to output variables such as shutter time, ray length, shaded area, UV derivatives, and so on as float values.

Surface Maps

Ambient Occlusion

Ambient Occlusion is not physically accurate like global illumination but it gives an approximation of global illumination. The **Ambient Occlusion** map produces realistic effect quickly.

This map shoots a number of rays in the upper hemisphere defined by the tangent plane of the shading point. Then, it returns the ratio of the hits divided by the total rays, as a color. The **White** parameter defines the output color when the ratio of the ray hits/total rays is **zero** (fully unoccluded). The **Black** parameter defines the output color when the ratio of the ray hits/total rays is **one** (fully occluded).

The **Samples** parameter defines the number of rays that will be fired to compute the hits/total ratio. The higher the value you specify, the better the quality will be. The images in Fig. 21 show the output with **Samples** set to **1** and **3**. Here, the **White** and

Black parameters were set to RGB [**0, 0.298, 0.788**] and RGB [**1, 1, 1**], respectively. Also, refer to the **ao-samples.max**.

The **Spread** parameter defines the angular spread around the normal vector in the range **0** to **1**. The value **1** represents the whole hemisphere [**90** degrees]. The images in Fig. 22 show the output with **Spread** set to **0, 0.5**, and **1**, respectively.

The **Near Clip** parameter defines the minimum occlusion distance that is sampled. The **Far Clip** parameter defines the minimum occlusion distance that is sampled. The images in Fig. 23 show the output with **Near Clip** set to **0, 1**, and **2**. The **Far Clip** were set to **10**. Also, refer to **ao-clipping.max**.

The **Falloff** parameter controls an exponential falloff rate for the occlusion along the ray distance. The **Normal** parameter alters the opacity of the ambient occlusion effect. As a result, the opacity of the object will be changed. The **Invert Normals** parameter is used to change the direction of the rays being used. One of the common use for this parameter is to simulate dirt and erosion. The **Self Only** check box allows you to gather occlusion against the shaded object only.

Complex Ior

The **Complex Ior** map can be used to render materials with complex index of refractions. The **Standard Surface** shader is used to calculate the Fresnel effect of the dielectric materials such as glass and plastic. However, metals have a more complex IOR that depends on another parameter called extinction coefficient.

Flakes

The **Flakes** map allows you to create flake normal map that you can use for materials such as car paint. A typical workflow would be to connect this map to the **normal** port of the **Standard Surface** shader.

 Caution: Noise in flakes
*There is no filtering algorithm associated with this map. Therefore, small flakes require more **AA** samples to become noise free. If you are rendering an animation using flakes, enable motion blur to avoid temporal flickering.*

The **Scale** parameter is used to scale the size of the flake structure up or down. Smaller values produce larger number of flakes. The images in Fig. 24 show the output with **Scale** set to **0.1, 0.05**, and **1**. Also, refer to **flakes-scale.max**.

The **Density** parameter controls the density of the flakes. There will be no flakes if you specify a value of **0** for this parameter. A value of **1** covers the whole surface with flakes. The images in Fig. 25 show the output with **Density** set to **0.1, 0.5**, and **1**. Also, refer to **flakes-density.max**.

The **Normal Randomize** parameter blends between the smooth surface normal and the random fake normal. The images in Fig. 26 show the output with **Normal Randomize** set to **0.1, 0.3**, and **0.6**. Also, refer to **flakes-normalize.max**.

The **Coord Space** parameter is used to specify the coordinate space used for calculating the shapes of the flakes. The following options are available: **world, object, Pref,** and **UV.** The **Output Space** parameter specifies the space of the output normal vector.

The **Step** and **Depth** parameters are used to control 3D flakes only. The **Flakes** map performs ray marching to compute 3D flakes. You can use the **Step** parameter to specify the step size. The number of layers is controlled by **Depth/Step** setting. The **Depth** parameter controls how deep a ray goes inside an object. When a ray hits an object, it can not traverse longer than the specified depth. The **IOR** parameter refracts a ray used for ray marching. You can use it to create a fake transparency effect.

Caution: 3D flakes and camera

*3D flakes will not render correctly if the camera is positioned inside a polymesh. Use smaller **Step** size if you are rendering flakes that are close to the camera so as not to miss any flakes. Also, note that by decreasing the **Step** value will dramatically increase render time.*

Shadow Matte

The **Shadow Matte** map is typically used to catch shadows on the floor planes from lighting within the scene. You can use this mat to render objects onto a photographic background. You can also render shadows separately for use in a compositing package.

Toon

The **Toon** map is used to render non-photorealistic images in combination with the **Contour** filter. The volumes, motion blur, DOF, and the VR camera do not currently work with the **Toon** map.

Texture Maps

Camera Projection

The **Camera Projection** map is used to perform camera projection of an image over an object. The output shown in the right image of Fig. 27 is produced by projecting the image shown in the left image. Refer to **camera-projection.max.**

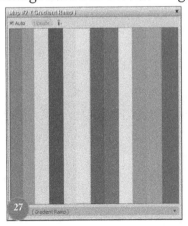

Cell Noise

The **Cell Noise** map is a pattern generator that you can use to create real-world patterns such as marble, granite, leather, and so on. The **Pattern** drop-down list provides seven cell patterns. The images in Fig. 28 show the output when **Pattern** is set to **noise1**, **noise2**, **cell1**, and **cell2**. The images in Fig. 29 show the output when **Pattern** is set to **worley1**, **worley2**, and **allegator**. Also, refer to the **cell-noise.max**.

On selecting the **Additive** check box, all noise patterns of different octaves are simple added. Otherwise, the largest value is selected. The images in Fig. 30 show with **Additive** disabled and enabled.

The **Octaves** parameter defines the number of octave over which the noise function is repeated. The images in Fig. 31 show the output when **Octaves** is set to **1, 2**, and **3**. Also, refer to **cell-octaves.max**.

The **Randomness** parameter controls how much the location of feature points is randomized. The **Lacunarity** [change in scale between each octave] parameter controls the average size of gaps in the texture pattern. In most cases, the default value if **1.92** will be suffice.

The **Amplitude** parameter defines the amplitude or range of the output. The images in Fig. 32 show the output when **Amplitude** is set to **0.1, 0.5,** and **1**. Also, refer to **amplitude-octaves.max**.

The **Color** parameter can be used to tint the noise. You can also connect a texture or ramp to the **Palette** parameter. The color will be randomly picked from the connected node by jittering UVs.

The **Density** parameter can only be used with the **cell1** and **cell2** patterns. It creates the flake noise by decimating some cells. The images in Fig. 33 show the output when **Density** is set to **0.25, 0.5,** and **0.75**. Also, refer to **amplitude-density.max**.

The options in the **Coord Space** drop-down list allow you to specify the coordinate space to use. The available options are **world, object, pref,** and **uv. Pref,** which is not really a space, but rather a reference to a bind pose. Also, note that **Pref** does not work with NURBS surfaces. Use the **Pref Name** parameter to specify the reference position user-data array which can be **RGB/RGBA** as well as **Vector**.

The **Scale** parameter controls the scale of the noise function in the x, y, and z directions. You can produce interesting results by scaling only in one direction. The images in Fig. 34 show output with **Scale** set to **[1, 0.1, 0.1], [0.1, 1.0, 0.1],** and **[0.1, 0.1, 1]**. Also, refer to **amplitude-scale-1.max, amplitude-scale-2.max,** and **amplitude-scale-3.max**. The **Offset** parameter is used to offset the noise in the x, y, or z directions.

The **P** parameter lets you specify the input coordinates of the noise function. Otherwise, the surface point is used. You can manually link a shader into this parameter to define an arbitrary coordinate space. The **Time** parameter is used to animate noise over time.

Checkerboard

The **Checkerboard** map is used to create a checkerboard pattern, refer to Fig. 35. Also, refer to **checkerboard-1.max**, **checkerboard-2.max**, and **checkerboard-3.max**.

Image

The **Image** map is used for texture mapping using an image file. You can use attributes [see Fig. 36] of this map to control the position, size, and rotation of the images on the surface.

The **Filename** parameter is used to specify an image as file texture. The options in the **Color Space** drop-down list are used to specify which color space the color texture is assumed to be in. The default option is **auto**. As a result, the colorspace will be guessed from the image properties. The **sRGB** colorspace will be used for 16-bit images, and **linear** otherwise.

The **Multiply** option multiplies the image by a constant. The left image in Fig. 37 shows the result with the default white color. The right image shows result when **Multiply** is set to red color. Also, refer to **image-multiply.max**.

The **Offset** parameter darkens or lightens the image uniformly. The options in the **Filter** drop-down list are used to select the **texel** interpolation method used to filter the rendered image. The **Mipmap Bias** parameter offsets the mip-map level from which a texture is sampled. Negative values result in sharper texture lookups. A positive value indicates a smaller mip-map level which produces a blurrier result. The images in Fig. 38 show output with **Mipmap Bias** set to **-5, 0,** and **5**. Also, refer to **image-mipmap.max**.

The **Single Channel** parameter reads and outputs the first channel of the image, which is usually the **Red** channel. You can override this behavior by specifying a channel using the **Start Channel** parameter. If you select the **Ignore Missing Textures** check box, Arnold does not generate an error when a missing file is encountered and displays the missing texture color specified using the **Missing Texture Color** parameter.

If you specify values for the **Custom UVs** parameter and if UV coordinates are linked to a shader, these values will be used as UV coordinates to sample the images, instead of the polymesh coordinates. In such a case, texture derivatives are not computed. As a result, destroying the texture mapping performance, especially in scenes with many, high resolution texture images.

You can select the UV set using the options available in the **UV Set** drop-down list. When **none** is selected, which is the default option, the primary UV set available in the polymesh will be used. The **Scale U** and **Scale V** parameters are used to scale the image along the U and V directions, respectively. The **Wrap U** and **Wrap V** parameters are used to specify how a texture repeats on a large surface along the U and V directions, respectively.

The **Swap U & V** check box is used to swap the axes. The **Flip U** check box flips the image in the horizontal direction whereas the **Flip V** check box flips the image in the vertical direction.

Layer Float

The **Layer Float** map allows you to combine up to 8 layers, linearly. Layers are applied in order.

Layer RGBA

The **Layer RGBA** map allows you to composite up to 8 shaders, enabling you to create complex shading effects. Layers are applied in order and combined using the blending mode. The blending mode is specified using the **Operation** drop-down list. You can also specify the original alpha value for the layer using the options available in the **Alpha Operation** drop-down list. Refer to **layer-rgba.max**.

Noise

The **Noise** map is used to calculate the coherent noise function. It produces output between 0 to 1. You can connect this map to other shader nodes to produce various effects. Also, refer to the **Cell Noise** section.

Ramp Float

The **Ramp Float** map allows to remap input value to a float value on a curve.

Ramp Rgb

The **Ramp Rgb** map allows to remap input value to an RGB color on curve. The **Ramp Float** and **Ramp Rgb** maps provide a gradient ramp for the RGB input and a spline ramp for the float output.

Triplanar

The **Triplanar** map allows you to quickly map a texture without using a UV map, by projecting it from all six sides.

User Data Maps

User Data Float

The **User Data Float** map reads float value from shape user data at the current shading point on the surface.

User Data Int

The **User Data Int** map reads integer value from shape user data at the current shading point on the surface.

User Data RGB

The **User Data RGB** map reads RGB color from shape user data at the current shading point on the surface.

User Data RGBA

The **User Data RGBA** map reads RGB color and alpha from shape user data at the current shading point on the surface.

User Data String

The **User Data String** map reads the string from shape user data.

Utility Maps

Blackbody

The **Blackbody** map emits a color based on the color temperature. You can use it for fire and explosions or for light emission using the blackbody spectrum. This shader is a copy of Houdini Pyro shader and thus tailored for the output of pyro simulations.

Cache

The **Cache** map allows you to avoid re-evaluating render-intensive part of the shading network. To use the cached result, the evaluations must share the same shading point, shading normal, ray origin, UVs, and geometry node.

Clamp

The **Clamp** map clamps the **Input** between the **Min** and **Max** values. Refer to **clamp.max**.

Curvature

The **Curvature** map outputs the curvature by sampling around the shading point within a given radius. This map is useful for creating procedural wear or dirt maps in conjunction with a **Noise** map.

The options in the **Output** drop-down list allow you to outputs result based on the concave and/or convex areas. This map outputs the **convex** and **concave** curvatures as grayscale values or output both with the **convex** curvature in the **red** channel and the **concave** curvature in the **green** channel. The images in Fig. 39 show the result with **Output** set to **convex, concave**, and **both**. Also, refer to **output-curvature.max**.

The **Samples** parameter controls the number of rays that will be fired to compute the curvature. The higher the value you specify, the less the noise will be, and the better the quality. The **Radius** parameter controls the radius of the sphere around the shading point within which the curvature will be estimated. The images in Fig. 40 show the result with **Radius** set to **0.1, 0.5,** and **1.**

The **Spread** parameter controls the directions of the rays. The default value of **1** means the rays are shot in all directions. Lower values of spread will shoot rays more vertically with respect to the surface. You can use this parameter to remove unwanted small variations of the curvature.

The **Threshold** parameter defines the normalized angle [**0** to **180** degrees]. Arnold considers curvature only above this value. This parameter is useful in pruning the geometry bubbles behind the surfaces of the convex curvature. The **Bias** parameter affects the falloff the curvature. The curvature is multiplied by the values of the **Multiply** parameter.

By default, the **Inclusive** check box is selected. It means that rays are tagged against tagged nodes as well as against the nodes that are not tagged at all. Otherwise, the rays are traced against all geometry except the tagged nodes. You can use the **Self Only** check box to limit the curvature sampling to the object being shaded.

Facing Ratio

The **Facing Ratio** map returns absolute value of the dot product [referred to as **incidence** in other renderers] between the shading normal and the incoming ray direction. This map works for any type of ray, not just camera rays. The returned values are always in the [0 .. 1] range. Refer to **facing-ratio.max.**

Flat

The **Flat** map outputs a color with no other effects.

Motion Vector

The **Motion Vector** map encodes a vector representing the motion of the object in the red and green components. To use this shader correctly, you need to enable motion blur in the render options and use an instantaneous shutter: the **shutter start/end** values should both be set to the same value.

Ray Switch RGBA

The **Ray Switch** map is used for evaluating different shader trees per ray. However, if you just want different color trees per ray, use can use the **Ray Switch RGBA** map. For example, if you want to give different appearance to an area which is behind a glass object, connect an input color to the **Specular Transmission** parameter of the **Ray Switch RGBA** map [see Fig. 41]. Also, refer to **ray-switch-rgba-map.max.**

Switch RGBA

The **Switch RGBA** map is used to switch between different colors. There are **20** ports [**input0** to **input19**] available on the **Switch RGBA** node. You can make a color active by entering its index number in the **Index** field. For example, if you want to make **input2** active, enter **1** in the **Index** field. Refer to **switch-rgba.max**.

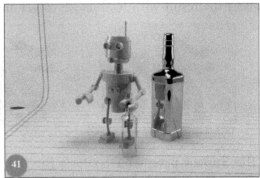

Utility

The **Utility** map is a general purpose utility node that can be used to create passes [AOVs] for use within a compositing package. It can be used for debugging the scenes. See **Unit A6 > Exercise 2** to understand the usage of the **Utility** map.

Uv Transform

You can use the **Uv Transform** map to modify UVs locally. It controls how a 2D texture is placed onto a surface. You can control the position, size, and scale of an image onto a surface.

Wireframe

The **Wireframe** map outputs a wire-frame style output as RGB. The options in the **Edge Type** drop-down define how the mesh is represented. When the **triangles** option is selected, polygons will be broken up into their triangular tessellation. The **polygons** option renders polygon faces as quads. The **patches** option is not currently supported.

Volume Maps

Volume Sample Float

The **Volume Sample Float** map samples volume channel of the new volume API. You need to connect it to the one of the components of the **Standard Volume** shader to further read values from a channel to apply different operations such as color correct. Both the **Volume Sample Float** and **Volume Sample RGB** maps share the same sampling controls, the only difference being the type of output, RGB or float.

Cryptomatte Map

The **Cryptomatte** map is an AOV shader which is used to encode Cryptomatte ID mattes into EXR outputs. See Unit A6 > Exercise 3 for more details about the functioning of the **Cryptomatte** map.

Hands-on Exercises

Exercise 1: Working with the Rounded Corners Map

In this exercise, we will work on the **Rounded Corners** map to give objects the appearance of rounded corners [see Fig. E1].

Table E1 summarizes the exercise.

Table E1	
Difficulty level	Intermediate
Estimated time to complete	25 Minutes
Topics in exercise	• Getting Started • Working On the Map
Resources folder	**unit-a4**
Start file	**rounded-corners-start.max**
Final exercise file	**rounded-corners-finish.max**

Getting Started

Open **rounded-corners-start.max** in 3ds Max and make sure the **Physical** camera is active.

Working On the Map

Follow these steps:

1. Open **Slate Material Editor** and then double-click on **standard-mat** swatch.

2. In the **Parameter Editor > Base** rollout > **Base Color** group, change **Base Weight** to **0.4**.

3. In the **Specular** rollout > **General** group, change **Roughness** to **0.4** and then in the **Advanced** group, change **Metalness** to **0.8**. Also, change **IOR** to **1.55** [see Fig. E2].

4. In **Slate Material Editor**, double-click on the **standard-mat** node > **normal** port to open **Material/Map Browser**. Double-click on **Bump2D** in the **Maps > Arnold > Bump** rollout.

5. In **Slate Material Editor**, double-click on the **Bump 2D** node > **bump_map** port to open **Material/Map Browser**. Double-click on **Noise** in the **Maps > General** rollout.

6. In the **Parameter Editor > Noise** map > **Coordinates** rollout, change **X Tiling** to **0**. In the **Noise Parameters** rollout, change **Noise Type** to **Regular, High** to **1, Low** to **0.255**, and **Size** to **0.1** [see Fig. E3].

What next?
*Notice in Fig. E3 that we need to fix the scale of the bump map to get the appearance right. We will do so by using the **Bump Height** parameter.*

7. In the **Parameter Editor > Bump 2D** map > **Parameters** rollout, change **Bump Height** to **0.02** [see Fig. E4].

What next?
*We have connected the output of the **Bump 2D** node to the **normal** port of the **standard-mat** node. Now, the **Round Corners** map has to be connected to the **normal** port of the **Standard Surface** node. We have to readjust the network for this arrangement.*

8. Disconnect the **Bump 2D** map and the **Standard Surface** shader nodes. Double-click on the **standard-mat** node > **normal** port to open **Material/Map Browser**. Double-click on **Rounded Corners** in the **Maps > Arnold > Bump** rollout. Now, connect **Bump 2D** output to the **normal** port of the **Rounded Corners** map [see Fig. E5].

9. In the **Parameter Editor > Round Corners** map > **Parameters** rollout, change **Samples** to **10** and **Radius** to **0.7** [see Fig. E6]. Fig. E7 shows the node network.

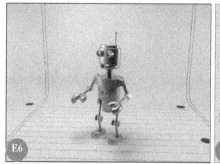

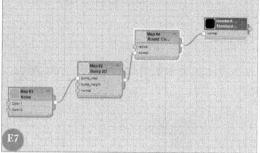

What next?

Now, create two emissive materials with red and green color. Apply red material to **Cylinder012, Cylinder013, Tube010,** *and* **Sphere008.** *Apply the green material to* **Sphere009** *[refer to Fig. E8].*

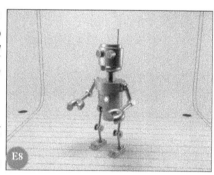

10. Press **F10** to open the **Render Setup** dialog box. In the **Arnold Renderer** panel > **Sampling and Ray Depth** rollout, change **Camera (AA), Diffuse,** and **Specular** samples to **5, 4,** and **4,** respectively. Render the scene [see Fig. E8].

Exercise 2: Working with the Color Correct Map

In this exercise, we will work on the **Color Correct** map [see Fig. E1]. We will create different textures for a wood shader using this map.

Table E2 summarizes the exercise.

Table E2	
Difficulty level	Intermediate
Estimated time to complete	20 Minutes
Topics in exercise	• Getting Started • Working On the Map
Resources folder	**unit-a4**
Start file	**color-correct-start.max**
Final exercise file	**color-correct-finish.max**

Getting Started
Open **color-correct-start.max** in 3ds Max and make sure the **Physical** camera is active.

Working On the Map
Follow these steps:

1. In the active view of **Slate Material Editor**, double-click on the **standard-mat** node > **base_color** port to open **Material/Map Browser**. Now, double-click on **Maps > General > Bitmap**. Select **wooden-plank-1.jpg** [see Fig. E2].

   → *What next?*
   *Next, we will create a grayscale map for the specular color using the **Color Correct** map.*

2. Double-click on the **standard-mat** node > **specular_color** port to open **Material/Map Browser**. Now, double-click on **Maps > Arnold > Color > Color Correct**. Now, connect the output of the **Bitmap** node to the **input** port of the **Color Correct** node. Fig. E3 shows the node network.

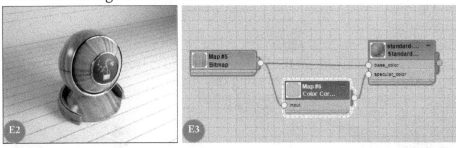

3. Double-click on the **Color Correct** node and then in the **Parameter Editor > Color** rollout, change **Saturation** to **0** and **Gamma** to **0.5** [see Fig. E4]. Now, connect output of the **Color Correct** node to the **standard-mat** node > **specular-roughness** port [see Fig. E5]. Fig. E6 shows the node network.

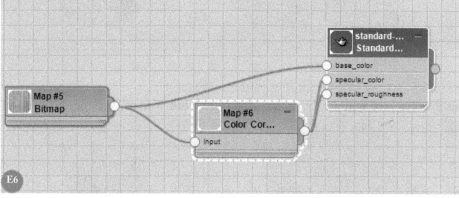

What next?

Notice in Fig. E5 that there is less shine on the wood. Next, we will modify the node network to make a shiny wood material.

4. Disconnect the **Color Correct** node and **specular_roughness** port of the **standard-mat** node. In the **Parameter Editor** > **Color Correct** node > **Color** rollout, change **Gamma** to **0.8** [see Fig. E7].

5. Create a copy of the **Color Correct** node using **Shift** and then connect its output to the **specular-roughness** port of the **standard-mat** node. In the **Parameter Editor** > new **Color Correct** node > **Color** rollout, change **Gamma** to **1** and **Exposure** to **-1** [see Fig. E8].

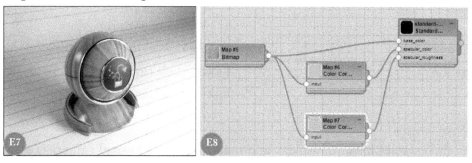

6. Add a **Bump 2D** node from the **Maps** > **Arnold** > **Bump** rollout. Make a connection between the new **Color Correct** node and the **bump_map** port of

the **Bump 2D** node. Now, connect output of the **Bump 2D** node to the **normal** port of the **standard-mat** port [see Fig. E9].

7. In the **Parameter Editor** > **Bump 2D** node > **Parameters** rollout, change **Bump Height** to **0.5** [see Fig. E10].

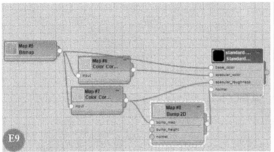 

Exercise 3: Working with the Flakes Map

In this exercise, we will create flakes using the **Flakes** map [see Fig. E1].

Table E3 summarizes the exercise.

Table E3	
Difficulty level	Intermediate
Estimated time to complete	20 Minutes
Topics in exercise	• Getting Started • Working with the Map
Resources folder	**unit-a4**
Start file	**flakes-start.max**
Final exercise file	**flakes-finish.max**

Getting Started

Open **flakes-start.max** in 3ds Max and make sure the **Physical** camera is active.

Follow these steps:

1. Open **Slate Material Editor** and then double-click on **standard-mat** swatch.

2. In the **Parameter Editor > Base** rollout > **Base Color** group, change **Base Weight** to **0.7** and **Base Color** to RGB [**0.953, 0.043, 0.043**].

3. In the **Specular** rollout > **General** group, change **Specular Color** to RGB [**0.082, 0.557, 0.396**]. In the **Advanced** group, change **IOR** to **5**, see Fig. E2.

4. In the **Coat** rollout, change **Coat Weight** to **1**. In the **Affect Underlying** group, change **Color** to **0.2**. In the **Thin Film** rollout, change **Thickness** to **500** [see Fig. E3].

5. Double-click on the **standard-mat** node > **normal** port to open **Material/Map Browser**. Now, double-click on **Maps > Arnold > Surface > Flakes** [see Fig. E4].

6. In the **Parameter Editor > Flakes** map > **Parameters** rollout, change **Scale** to **0.05**, **Density** to **0.3**, and **Normal Randomize** to **0.6** [see Fig. E5].

Quiz

Multiple Choice
Answer the following questions, only one choice is correct.

1. Which of the following nodes is available in **Bump** maps category?

   [A] Bump 2D   [B] Normal 2D
   [C] Bump 3D   [D] Round Corners

2. Which of the following **Conversion** maps is available in Arnold?

   [A] Float to RGB   [B] Float to RGBA
   [C] Vector to RGBA   [C] Vector Map

Fill in the Blanks
Fill in the blanks in each of the following statements:

1. The _____ map allows you to give appearance of a round corner near the edges by modifying the shading normals.

2. You can use the _____ input port of the **Round Corners** map to chain multiple bump maps.

3. The _____ map allows you to convert an input color to RGB color space, to HSV color space, and vice-versa.

4. The _____ map is used to adjust the gamma, hue, saturation, contrast, and exposure of an input image.

5. The _____ map returns the following value: (**1 - Input**). You can use this map to invert an image.

6. The _____ map returns the following value: **Input 1 * Input 2**.

7. You can use the _____ map to output shading normals, including smooth normals, and bump maps as vectors.

8. The _____ map is a pattern generator that you can use to create real-world patterns such as marble, granite, leather, and so on.

9. The _____ map outputs the curvature by sampling around the shading point within a given radius.

10. The _____ map returns absolute value of the dot product [referred to as incidence in other renderers] between the shading normal and the incoming ray direction.

True or False
State whether each of the following is true or false:

1. The **Round Corners** map will not work correctly if the normals are not correctly oriented on the object.

2. The **Round Corners** map does not work with displacement.

3. The normal AOV [**N**] can be used to check how the **Round Corners** map rounds the shading normals.

4. The **Modulo** map returns **Division** modulo **Input**.

5. The **Random** map is used to output a random color from various types of inputs.

6. 3D flakes will not render correctly if the camera is positioned inside a polymesh.

7. The **Layer RGBA** map allows you to combine up to **8** layers, linearly.

8. The **Flat** map outputs a color with no other effects.

9. The **Motion Vector** map encodes a color representing the motion of the object in the red and green components.

10. You can use the **Uv Transform** map to modify UVs locally.

Summary

In this unit, the following topics are covered:

- Arnold Maps

Unit A5: Cameras

Cameras present a scene from a particular point of view. Camera objects in 3ds Max simulate still-image, motion picture, or video cameras in real-world. With a **Camera** viewport you can adjust the camera as if you were looking through its lens. Currently, only basic features are supported by the Arnold cameras. Full support for the Arnold's cameras will be available in future releases. The following camera types are available in Arnold:

- **VR Camera**
- **Fisheye**
- **Cylindrical**
- **Spherical**

3ds Max's **Physical** camera is supported by Arnold. The **Physical** camera is used to integrate framing the scene with exposure control and other effects that model real-world cameras. In this unit, we will discuss about **Physical** camera and camera effects.

Exposure Controls in Real-World Cameras

3ds Max emulates the real-world cameras to help you create physically accurate lighting and render realistic looking images. In order to create accurate lighting, you need to understand the terms shutter speed and aperture. They are used to control the amount of light in the scene as well as the focus effects such as depth-of-field.

Aperture

In optics, an aperture is a hole that allow you to control the amount of light passing through the lens of a camera. It controls the cone angle of a group of rays that come to a focus in the image plane. The term f-stop [sometimes also referred to as called focal ratio, f-ratio, f-stop, or relative aperture] is used for the quantitative measure of lens speed. The widest apertures have f-stops with the smallest numbers. The maximum aperture available is dependent on the lens you are using. The standard f-stop values are: f1.8, f2.8, f4, f5.6, f8, f11, and f16 [refer to Fig. 1].

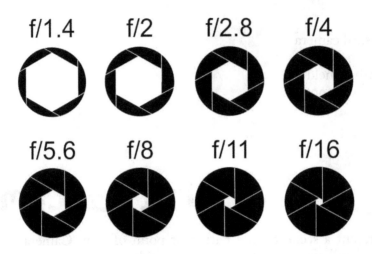

The aperture can also be used for controlling the depth-of-field effect. This effect is generated by focusing on a fixed point [called focal plane] in a scene. The group around the plane remains in focus whereas the rest is blurred. You can get higher blurring using wider apertures [smaller f-stop values]. If the aperture is very small, the depth of field will be large whereas if the aperture is large, the depth of field will be small.

Note: Lens opening
An iris diaphragm is used to control the opening of the lens.

Shutter Speed

The shutter speed or exposure time is the length of time, the shutter of the camera is open when taking a photograph. In other words, the shutter speed controls the length of a time a film sensor is exposed. The shutter speed is measured in seconds, mostly in fractions of seconds, for example, 1/512. Bigger the denominator, faster the speed.

Tip: Shutter speed
To know more about shutter speed, visit the following link:
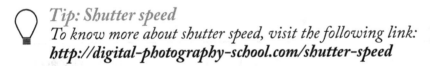
http://digital-photography-school.com/shutter-speed

When shutter speed is fast, a small amount of light travels and visa-versa. Generally, you are required to adjust both the aperture and shutter speed to ensure that correct amount of light travels through. Slow shutter speeds allow more light into sensor and are used for low light or night photography. The faster shutter speed helps to freeze the motion.

Below are some possibilities:

- On a sunny bright day, you will use a faster shutter speed [1/250s] and small aperture [f/11] to compensate for the bright outdoor light.
- On a cloudy day, reduce the speed so that more light hits the sensor [1/100s, f11].
- If the scene contains a fast moving object, use the faster shutter speed [to prevent blurring]. You are required to open the aperture to let in more light [1/500s, f/2.8].

ISO

ISO is the level of sensitivity of the camera to the available light. It is measured in numbers. A lower number represents lower sensitivity to the available light whereas higher numbers mean more sensitivity. As the ISO increases, the grain or noise in the image also increases. The examples of ISO are: **100, 200, 400, 800**, and **1600**.

 How Aperture, Shutter Speed, and ISO work together?
Here's what happens when you click the shutter release button:

1. *You point you camera to the subject and press the shutter button.*
2. *The subject enters into the camera in form of light.*
3. *The light passed through various optical elements and then goes through the lens.*
4. *Light hits the aperture curtain.*
5. *Shutter opens for some milliseconds.*
6. *Light hits the sensor for the specified time [shutter speed]*
7. *Sensor gathers the light based on a pre-defined sensitivity [ISO].*
8. *Shutter closed and light is blocked from reaching the camera sensor.*

As you can see the aperture, shutter speed, and ISO work together to create exposure for the images. When you are lighting your scene in 3ds Max, you are required to experiment with different numbers to obtain correct lighting condition.

Exposure Controls

3ds Max provides different controls for adjusting the output levels and color range for a scene. The process for adjusting the levels is known as tone mapping. This process compensates for the limited dynamic range of the computer display in comparison to the human eye. The exposure controls adjust the colors so that they are close to the dynamic range of the human eye.

You can adjust the exposure using the options available in the **Exposure Control** rollout. The path to access this rollout is as follows: **Rendering** menu > **Exposure Control**. The exposure controls included with 3ds Max are: **Automatic Exposure**

Control, Linear Exposure Control, Logarithmic Exposure Control, Physical Camera Exposure Control, and Pseudo Color Exposure Control.

You can use the **Automatic Exposure Control** for preparing the first draft of the rendering. It is also useful in rendering still images. If the primary light source in your scene are standard lights instead of photometric lights, use the **Logarithmic Exposure Control**. If you are dealing with scenes that have the moving camera, use the **Logarithmic Exposure Control**. Use the **Physical Camera Exposure Control** to render high dynamic range images using **Physical** camera.

Figure 2 shows the **Exposure Control** rollout. You can use the drop-down list available in this rollout to select the exposure control that you want to use. The **Active** check box when selected, the selected exposure control from the drop-down list is used by 3ds Max.

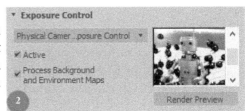

If you want to affect the scene background and environment maps, select the **Process Background and Environment Maps** check box. To preview the render of the scene with the selected exposure control applied, click **Render Preview**. The preview thumbnail appears above the button, see Fig. 2.

Physical Camera

The **Physical** camera is used to create photorealistic physically-based renderings. To create a **Physical** camera, in the **Create** panel, click **Cameras**, and then select **Standard** from the drop-down list below **Cameras**, if not already selected. Now, in the **Object Type** rollout, click **Physical** and then click-drag in a viewport to place the camera. To display the camera view, press **C** on the keyboard. The parameters associated with the **Physical** camera are discussed next.

Basic Rollout
The **Targeted** check box is selected by default. It is used to specify that the camera has a target. The **Target Distance** parameter controls the distance between the target and the focal plane. The options in the **Show Cone** drop-down list let you specify whether the camera cone will be displayed always, never, or on selection. The **Show Horizon Line** check box displays the horizontal line in the **Camera** viewport.

Physical Camera Rollout
The options in the **Preset** drop-down list are used to specify the film sensor of the camera. The **Width** parameter allows you to specify a custom film sensor width. If you specify a custom value for this parameter, **Preset** will change to **Custom**. The **Focal Length** parameter is used to specify the focal length of lens. The default value is **40**.

If you select the **Specify FOV** check box, the **Focal Length** parameter will be disabled. You can use the **Specify FOV** parameter to specify the new field-of-view in degrees. Use the **Zoom** parameter to adjust the zoom level of camera without changing its position.

The **Aperture** parameter allows you to set the aperture as an f-number or f-stop. The **Use Target Distance** parameter is used to set the focal distance same as the target distance specified using the **Target Distance** parameter. If you want the focal distance to be different than the target distance, select the **Custom** option; the **Focus Distance** parameter will be activated.

The **Lens Breathing** parameter is used to move the lens toward the focal distance or away from it to adjust the field-of-view. The **Enable Depth of Field** check box, when selected, enables the depth-of-field effect based on the **Aperture** setting. The blurring occurs at a distance which is not equal to **Focus Distance**.

The options in the **Type** drop-down list are used to specify the unit for the shutter speed. The **Duration** parameter is used to define the shutter speed. The duration depends on the type of unit specified in the **Type** drop-down list. Select the check box below the **Duration** parameter to enable the **Offset** parameter. The **Offset** parameter lets you define the timing of the opening of the shutter related to the start of each frame. The timing is dependent on the option that you select from the **Type** drop-down list. Select **Enable Motion Blur** check box to generate the motion blur effect.

Exposure Rollout

If exposure is already activated for the **Physical** camera, the **Exposure Control Installed** button in this rollout is deactivated and the label of the button reads "**Exposure Control Installed**". Also, the **Physical Camera Exposure Control** option is selected in the drop-down list available in the **Environment and Effects** window > **Exposure Control** rollout [see Fig. 3].

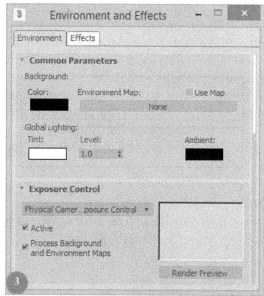

If you select the option other than the **Physical Camera Exposure Control** option in this drop-down list, the **Exposure Control Installed** button changes to the **Install Exposure Control** button and the other parameters in the **Exposure** rollout are deactivated.

Now, if you click the **Install Exposure Control** button, the **Physical Camera Exposure Control** message box will be displayed. Choose **OK**; the **Physical Camera Exposure Control** option will be selected in the **Environment and Effects** window > **Exposure Control** rollout replacing the currently selected exposure option.

When you select **Manual**, the field next to it will be activated. You can use the value in this field to set exposure gain via an ISO value. The exposure value is directly proportional to the value you specify for this parameter. The **Target** option is selected by default. The higher the value you specify for this parameter, the lesser will be the exposure value [**EV**].

The **Illuminant** option is selected by default in the **White Balance** group. As a result, the drop-down list below it is active. The options in this drop-down list consist of various options to adjust the color balance. The color swatch next to it changes based on the option selected in the drop-down list and sets the color balance accordingly.

If you select the **Temperature** option, the field below it will be activated. The color swatch next to it changes depending on the value set in the field and is used to set the color balance in terms of color temprature. If you select the **Custom** option, the color swatch below it will be activated. You can set the color in this color swatch to set the color balance. Select the **Enable Vignetting** check box, to activate the **Amount** parameter. The higher the value you specify for the **Amount** parameter, more will be the vignetting effect. This effect results in darkness at the edges of the film plane at rendering.

Bokeh (Depth of Field) Rollout
When the **Enable Depth of Field** check box is selected in the **Physical Camera** rollout, a pattern is created in the groups of the image that are out of focus. This is known as **Bokeh** effect.

The parameters in the **Aperture Shape** group defines the shape of the bokeh pattern. The default option **Circular** means that a circular shaped pattern will be created. If you select the **Bladed** option, the sharp edge shaped pattern is created in which the number of edges in the shape depend on the value you specify for the **Blades** parameter. The **Rotation** parameter is used to specify the angle of rotation for all shapes in the pattern.

 Caution: Arnold and Physical camera
*The rest of parameters [in the **Bokeh (Depth of Field)** rollout] discussed next are not currently supported by Arnold. Full support for the Arnold's cameras will be available in future releases.*

If you select the **Custom Texture** option, you can specify a map using the **No Map** button. This map replaces the shape in a pattern. The slider in the **Center Bias (Ring Effect)** group biases the transparency of the aperture toward the center [negative values] or the edge [positive values]. Positive values increase the amount of blurring in out-of-focus areas, while negative values decrease the blur.

The slider in the **Optical Vignetting (Cat Eye)** group allows you to simulate the "cat's eye" effect that some wide-angle lenses can generate. The slider in the **Anisotropy (Anamorphic Lens)** group lets you simulate an anamorphic lens by stretching the aperture vertically [negative values] or horizontally [positive values].

Perspective Control Rollout

The parameters in **Lens Shift** group are used to move the camera view horizontally or vertically without changing its position or orientation. The parameters in the **Tilt Correction** group are used to tilt the camera horizontally or vertically and to correct the perspective. The **Auto Vertical Tilt Correction** check box is used to auto correct the tilt correction along the Z axis.

Lens Distortion Rollout

The **None** option is selected by default in the **Distortion Type** Group. As a result, there is no distortion applied. Select the **Cubic** option; the **Amount** parameter will be activated. The positive value in this parameter results in pincushion distortion whereas negative value in this parameter results in barrel distortion.

If you select the **Texture** option, the **No Map** button will be activated. Use this button to link a map. The distortion of the image depends on the colors in the linked image.

Miscellaneous Rollout

Select the **Enable** check box in the **Clipping Planes** group to add near and far clipping planes. Specify the distance of the near clipping plane from the camera in the **Near** field and the distance of the far clipping plane from the camera in the **Far** field. Note that the objects in between the camera and the near clipping plane and the objects which are outside the far clipping plane will not be visible in renderings.

Hands-on Exercises

Exercise 1: Working with the Depth-of-Field Effect

In this exercise, we will work on the depth-of-field effect using the **Physical** camera [see Fig. E1].

Table E1 summarizes the exercise.

Table E1	
Difficulty level	Intermediate
Estimated time to complete	25 Minutes
Topics in exercise	• Getting Started • Working On the Effect
Resources folder	**unit-a5**
Start file	**dof-start.max**
Final exercise file	**dof-finish.max**

Getting Started
Open **dof-start.max** in 3ds Max.

Working On the Effect
Follow these steps:

1. Make sure the **Physical** camera is selected and active. Fig. E2 shows the camera in the **Top** viewport.

2. In the **Modify** panel > **Basic** rollout, change **Target Distance** to **530** [see Fig. E3].

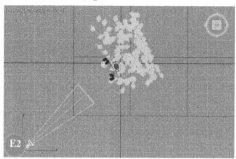 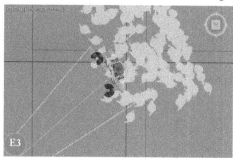

 What just happened?
Here, we want to focus on the robot and this is the reason we have moved focal point to the robot in the scene. The **Target Distance** parameter controls the distance between the target and the focal plane. This parameter affects focusing, depth-of-field, and so on.

Notice in the **Physical Camera** rollout > **Focus** group, the **Use Target Distance** radio button is selected. As a result, the focus distance will be controlled by the **Target Distance** parameter. You can also specify a custom focus distance by selecting the **Custom** radio button and then specifying a value for the **Focus Distance** parameter.

3. In the **Physical Camera** rollout > **Focus** group, select the **Enable Depth of Field** check box.

 What just happened?
Here, by selecting the **Enable Depth of Field** check box, 3ds Max will generate blurring at distances not equal to the focus distance. The amount of blurring will be controlled by the **Aperture** setting.

 Note: Exposure
Notice in the **Exposure** rollout > **Exposure Gain** group, we have defined exposure using a **EV** value. Therefore, when we will change the **Aperture** setting for controlling the depth–of–field effect, the scene's exposure will not be affected.

What next?
Notice in Fig. E4, there is no depth-of-field effect visible in the render. Next, we will change the **Aperture** settings to create the effect.

4. In the **Modify** panel > **Physical Camera** rollout > **Lens** group, change **Aperture** to **0.1** [see Fig. E5].

> **What just happened?**
> *Here, we have set aperture as f-number or f-stop. The lower the f-number you specify, the wider the aperture and the narrower the depth-of-field will be.*

5. Change **Aperture** to **1** [see Fig. E6]. Change **Aperture** to **5** [see Fig. E7]. Change **Aperture** to **2.2** [see Fig. E8].

What next?

*Notice in the **Bokeh (Depth of Field)** rollout > **Aperture Shape** group, the **Circular** radio button is selected. This default setting means that the Bokeh effect will be based on a circular aperture [see Fig. E8]. You can also use a aperture with edges using the **Bladed** parameter. Let's see how it looks.*

6. Select the **Bladed** radio button and then change **Blades** to **3** and **Rotation** to **90** [see Fig. E9].

7. Press **F10** to open the **Render Setup** dialog box. In the **Arnold Renderer** panel > **Sampling and Ray Depth** rollout, change **Camera (AA), Diffuse,** and **Specular** samples to **5, 4,** and **4,** respectively. Render the scene.

Exercise 2: Working with the Motion Blur Effect

In this exercise, we will work on the motion blur effect using the **Physical** camera as well as using Arnold's native motion blur settings [see Fig. E1]. Table E2 summarizes the exercise.

Table E2	
Difficulty level	Intermediate
Estimated time to complete	25 Minutes
Topics in exercise	• Getting Started • Working On the Effect
Resources folder	**unit-a4**
Start file	**dof-start.max**
Final exercise file	**dof-finish.max**

Getting Started

Open **dof-start.max** in 3ds Max. This file contains an animated object from frame **0** to frame **100**.

Working On the Effect

Follow these steps:

1. Make sure the **Physical** camera is selected and active.

2. In the **Modify** panel > **Physical Camera** rollout > **Shutter** group, select the **Enable Motion Blur** check box. Go to the frame **50** in the timeline and then render the scene [see Fig. E2].

   ? *What just happened?*
   *By selecting the **Enable Motion Blur** check box, we have ensured that the camera generates motion blur. We can control motion blur using the shutter speed which is defined using the **Duration** and **Offset** settings. The default duration is **0.5** frame.*

3. Change **Duration** to **10** [see Fig. E3]. Change **Duration** to **5** [see Fig. E4]. Change **Duration** to **2** [see Fig. E5].

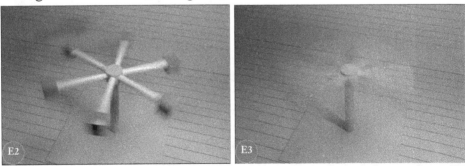

   ? *What next?*
   Notice in Fig. E5 that the output is not representing the motion trail of the curvy motion, the trail is looking more like a box trail. Next, we will fix it using render settings.

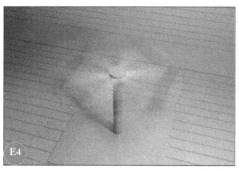

4. Press **F10** to open the **Render Setup** window.

 Note: Transform keys
*Notice in the **Arnold Renderer** panel > **Motion Blur** rollout, the **Transform Keys** parameter is set to **2**. This parameter defines the number of sub-steps used for the motion blur.*

5. Change **Transform Keys** to **4** [see Fig. E6].

Note: Memory usage
*Increasing the value of the **Transform Keys** parameter does not usually have much effect on the rendering time, although it requires more memory to store the additional geometry at multiple times [especially for large polygon meshes]. The effect of this parameter is more apparent when calculating motion blur for a deforming object along a motion path.*

 Note: Deform Keys parameter
If you are creating the motion blur effect for objects such as hair or grass, you require deformation keys.

Note: Motion blur and Camera settings
*If you clear the **Respect Physical Camera settings** check box, Arnold will ignore the camera settings and use the settings you specify in the **Motion Blur** rollout to create the blur effect.*

6. Clear the **Respect Physical Camera settings** check box. Now, if you render the scene, you will notice there is no effect available. Select the **Transform Keys** check box. If you render the scene now [see Fig. E7], you will see that the motion blur effect is back in the render.

7. In the **Motion Blur Time Span** group, change **Length** to **1** [see Fig. E8].

Parameter: Length

*The **Length** parameter is used to tweak the size and length of the motion blur trails. The **0**, **0.5**, and **1** values for this parameter represent **0**, **180**, and **360** degrees shutter angles, respectively. Normally the value of the **Length** parameter won't be bigger than one frame unless you are looking for an exaggerated effect. Fig. E9 show the result with **Length** set to **5**. The options in the drop-down list located to the right of the **Length** parameter define an offset for the shutter's time interval. These option allow you change the motion blur trails.*

8. Change **Length** to **2** and **Shutter Type** to **Box** [see Fig. E10]. Change **Shutter Type** to **Triangle** [see Fig. E11]. Change **Shutter Type** to **Curve** and then modify the curve, as shown in Fig. E12. Render the scene [see Fig. E13].

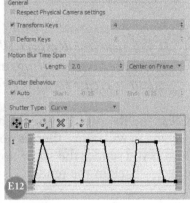

What just happened?
*While computing the motion blur effect, filtering is applied to the time samples. By default, the **Box** filter is applied to samples which essentially means that all time samples have the same weight. The **Triangle** filter produces smoother trails. You can also create custom shutter shape using the **Curve** filter [refer to E12].*

Quiz

Multiple Choice
Answer the following questions, only one choice is correct.

1. Which of the following cameras is not available in Arnold?

   [A] VR Camera   [B] Fisheye
   [C] Cylindrical   [D] Conical

2. Which of the following terms represents the level of sensitivity of the camera to the available light?

   [A] Shutter Speed   [B] Aperture
   [C] ISO   [D] F-Stop

3. Which of the following exposure controls is not available in 3ds Max?

   [A] Linear Exposure Control   [B] Logarithmic Exposure Control
   [C] Physical Camera Exposure Control [D] mr Photographic Exposure Control

Fill in the Blanks
Fill in the blanks in each of the following statements:

1. In optics, an _____ is a hole that allow you to control the amount of light passing through the lens of a camera.

2. The _____ parameter controls the distance between the target and the focal plane.

3. The **Use Target Distance** parameter is used to set the focal distance same as the target distance specified using the _____ parameter.

4. The **Enable Depth of Field** check box, when selected, enables the depth-of-field effect based on the _____ setting.

5. The _____ parameter is used to define the shutter speed.

True or False
State whether each of the following is true or false:

1. The widest apertures have f-stops with the smallest numbers.

2. The depth-of-field effect is generated by focusing on a fixed point [called focal plane] in a scene.

3. The aperture controls the length of a time a film sensor is exposed.

4. As you can see the aperture, shutter speed, and ISO work together to create exposure for the images.

Summary
In this unit, the following topics are covered:

- Physical camera
- Motion Blur
- Depth of field
- Exposure controls

Unit A6: Arnold Render Settings

When Arnold is the currently selected renderer in 3ds Max, you can access Arnold render settings from the **Render Setup** window. These are global settings that control the behavior of Arnold rendering. You can access global render settings by choosing **Render Setup** from the **Rendering** menu or by pressing **F10**. In this unit, we will discuss various AOVs provided by Arnold.

AOVs

AOVs [Arbitrary Output Variables] are similar in concept to **Render Elements** in 3ds Max and allow you to render any arbitrary shading network component into different images and then you can use them to composite the final image. Arnold provides the following built-in system AOVs. These AOVs are always available, no matter what shader(s) are you using. Table 1 summarizes the AOVs:

Table 1: List of AOVs	
AOV	**Description**
A	Alpha
AA_inv_density	You can use this AOV with a heatmap filter to visualize the sample density with Adaptive Sampling.
ID	It outputs a random number value derived from the name of the shape. You can also add specific ID numbers via the user options string field for an object.
N	It outputs the smooth normal at shading point in the world space.
Pref	It outputs reference position of the shading point.
RGBA	It outputs full rendered image, the beauty pass.

Table 1: List of AOVs

AOV	Description
Z	It outputs depth of the shading point as seen from the camera.
albedo	It outputs reflectivity, the surface or volume color without lighting or shadowing.
background	It outputs emission from the background and skydome lights visible to the camera.
coat	It outputs coat reflection.
coat_albedo	It outputs coat color without lighting or shadowing.
coat_direct	It outputs coat direct lighting.
coat_indirect	It outputs coat indirect lighting.
cputime	It outputs the CPU time [measured in "ticks"] to evaluate the samples in the pixel.
diffuse	It outputs diffuse reflection.
diffuse_albedo	It outputs diffuse color without lighting or shadowing.
diffuse_direct	It outputs diffuse direct lighting.
diffuse_indirect	It outputs diffuse indirect lighting.
direct	It outputs direct lighting from all surfaces and volumes.
emission	It outputs lights and emissive objects directly visible from the camera.
indirect	It outputs indirect light from all surfaces and volumes.
motionvector	It outputs a 2D vector representing the motion in the screen space of the shading point. If output to an **RGB** format, the vector is contained in the **R** and **G** channels.
opacity	It outputs to RGB with full three-channel opacity (as opposed to single channel alpha).
raycount	It outputs the total number of rays traced for samples in the pixel.
shadow_matte	It outputs shadows in the scene. They are computed as the ratio of occluded direct lighting over unoccluded direct lighting.
specular	It outputs specular reflection.
specular_albedo	It outputs the specular color without lighting or shadowing.
specular_direct	It outputs specular direct lighting.
specular_indirect	It outputs specular indirect lighting.
sss	It outputs subsurface scattering and diffuse transmission.

Table 1: List of AOVs	
AOV	**Description**
sss_albedo	It outputs SSS and diffuse transmission color without lighting or shadowing.
sss_direct	It outputs SSS and diffuse transmission direct lighting.
sss_indirect	It outputs SSS and diffuse transmission indirect lighting.
transmission	It outputs specular transmission [refraction].
transmission_albedo	It outputs specular transmission color without lighting or shadowing.
transmission_direct	It outputs specular transmission direct lighting.
transmission_indirect	It outputs specular transmission indirect lighting.
volume	It outputs volume scattering.
volume_z	It outputs the Z depth for the first volume contribution in a flat AOV.
volume_albedo	It outputs volume color without lighting or shadowing.
volume direct	It outputs volume scatter direct lighting.
volume indirect	It outputs volume scatter indirect lighting.
volume opacity	It outputs to RGB with the full three-channel opacity for volumes only.

Note: Other AOV groups

*The other AOV groups correspond to the shader nodes being used. For example, the **Shadow Matte** provides the following AOVs: **shadow**, **shadow diff**, and **shadow mask**.*

Note: Multiple shaders

*Multiple shaders in the scene can contribute to the same AOV. For example, the **Standard Surface** shader and the **Lambert** shader, both write to the **diffuse_direct** AOV.*

AOV Settings

You can adjust AOV settings from the **AOVs** panel of the **Render Setup** window. You can select the AOV output file from the **File Type (driver)** drop-down list. You can select one of the following formats: **DeepEXR**, **EXR**, **Jpeg**, **Png**, and **Tiff**.

Caution: EXR Files

3ds Max does not support more recent multi-layer EXR format natively. EXRs with only one layer should work fine.

Cryptomatte

Arnold for 3ds Max supports **Cryptomatte**, an ID matte creation tool created by Jonah Friedman. This tool creates ID mattes automatically. These mattes support motion effects such as motion blur, depth-of-field, and transparency. The following **Cryptomatte** AOVs are available in Arnold:

- **crypto_asset:** It creates the same matte for all assets.
- **crypto_material:** It creates a matte based on the assigned shader.
- **crypto_object:** It creates a matte based on the object name.

Hands-on Exercises

Exercise 1: Working with AOVs

In this exercise, we will work on AOVs [refer to Fig E1].

Table E1 summarizes the exercise.

Table E1	
Difficulty level	Intermediate
Estimated time to complete	45 Minutes
Topics in exercise	• Getting Started • Working On AOVs
Resources folder	**unit-a6**
Start file	**aovs-start.max**
Final exercise file	**aovs-finish.max**

Getting Started

Open **aovs-start.max** in 3ds Max and make sure **Physical** camera is active.

Working On AOVs

Follow these steps:

1. Press **F10** to open the **Render Setup** window. Switch to the **AOVs** panel [see Fig. E2]. In this panel, make sure **EXR** is selected in the **File Type (driver)** drop-down list and then click on the **Add AOV File** button.

What just happened?
*On clicking the **Add AOV File** button, the available AOVs appear in the list box in the **AOVs** panel [see Fig. E3]. Now, we can choose the AOVs that we want to render from the **builtin** group.*

2. Expand the **builtin** group and then choose **diffuse, diffuse_albedo, diffuse_direct, diffuse_indirect,** and **direct** using the **Ctrl** key [**Shift** to select a range] and then click the **Add** button; the selected AOVs appear in the list box [see Fig. E4].

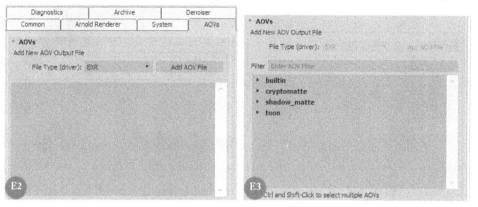

Note: Removing AOVs
*If you want to remove all AOVs from a group, select the header **AOVs (EXR)** in the list box and then click **Remove**. To remove an individual AOV, select it in the list box and then click **Remove**. When you select the group header, you can change the format settings from the **Output File Settings** group of the **AOVs** rollout [see Fig. E5].*

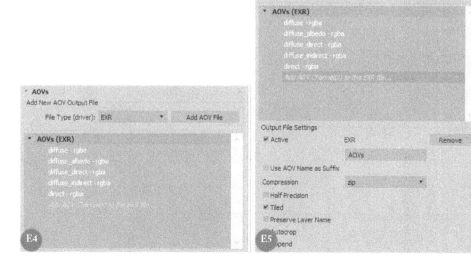

3. Render the scene. Fig. E6 shows the **RGBA** AOV. Fig. E7 through E11 show the **diffuse, diffuse_albedo, diffuse_direct, diffuse_indirect,** and **direct** AOVs, respectively.

4. Click on **AOVs (EXR) > Add AOV Channel(s) to this EXR file** and then choose **indirect, N, coat, coat_albedo, coat_direct, coat_indirect, object, P, shader, shadow_matte, specular, specular_albedo, specular_direct, specular_indirect, sss, sss_albedo, sss_direct, sss_indirect, transmission, transmission_albedo, transmission_indirect, volume, volume_albedo, volume_direct, volume_opacity,** and **volume_Z** from the **builtin** group. Now, click **Add**. The following table summarizes the AOVs and Figs. Also, refer to **aovs-finish.max**.

Table E1.1	
Fig. Number	AOV
7	diffuse
8	diffuse_albedo
9	diffuse_direct
10	diffuse_indirect
11	direct
12	indirect
13	N
14	coat
15	coat_albedo
16	coat_direct

Table E1.1	
Fig. Number	AOV
17	coat_indirect
18	object
19	P
20	shader
21	shadow_matte
22	specular
23	specular_albedo
24	specular_direct
24A	specular_indirect
25	SSS
26	sss_albedo
27	sss_direct
28	sss_indirect
29	transmission
30	transmission_albedo
31	transmission_indirect
32	volume
33	volume_albedo
34	volume_direct
35	volume_opacity
36	volume_Z

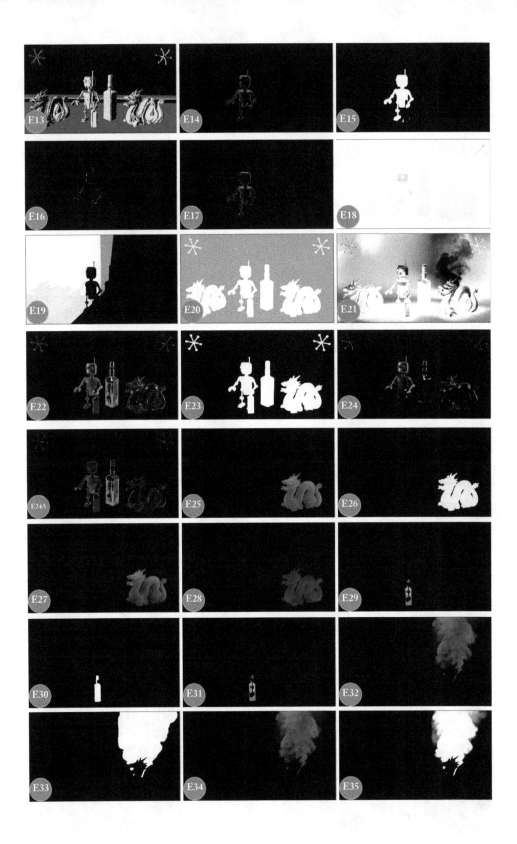

What next?
Next, we will work on creating custom AOVs. You can use the custom AOVs, if you want to render a custom effect that is not available from the existing AOV list. Next, we will create a wireframe AOV for the bottle in the scene.

5. Open **aovs-start-1.max**. Open **Slate Material Editor**. Frame the **chrome-mat** node in the active view.

6. RMB click in the active view and then choose **Maps > Arnold > Utility > Wireframe**; a **Wireframe** node is added to the active view.

7. RMB click in the active view and then choose **Materials > Arnold > AOV > AOV Write RGB**; a **AOV Write RGB** node is added to the active view.

8. Connect **chrome-mat** with the **passthrough** port of the **AOV Write RGB** node and then connect **Wireframe** node with the **aov_input** port of the **AOV Write RGB** node. Fig. E37 shows the node network.

9. In the **Parameter Editor > AOV Write RGB > Parameters** rollout, change **AOV Name** to **wireframePass**. Now, assign **AOV Write RGB** to the bottle in the scene.

10. Press **F10** to open the **Render Setup** window. In the **AOVs** panel, click **AOVs (EXR) > Add AOV Channel(s) to this EXR file**. Now, change **Enter Custom AOV Name** [see Fig. E38] to **wireframePass** and then click the **Add to List** button; **wireframePass** appears under the custom group in the list box [see Fig. E39].

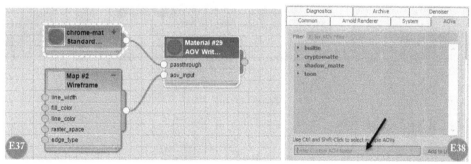

11. Make sure **wireframePass** is selected in the list box and then click the **Add** button to add **wireframePass** to the **AOVs (EXR)** group [see Fig. E40]. Render the scene. Fig. E41 shows the **wireframePass** AOV. Also, refer to **aovs-start-1-finish.max**.

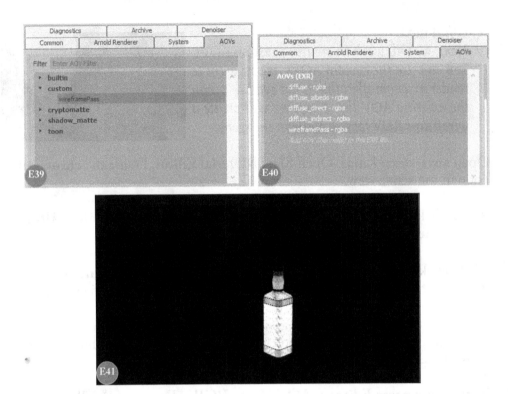

Exercise 2: Working with AOVs

In Exercise 1, we created a wireframe AOV for the bottle. We can also create multiple AOVs for an object in the scene. In this exercise, we will create additional object AOV for the bottle mesh using the **Passthrough** shader [see Fig. E1].

Table E2 summarizes the exercise.

Table E2	
Difficulty level	Intermediate
Estimated time to complete	15 Minutes
Topics in exercise	• Getting Started • Working On the Passthrough Shader
Resources folder	**unit-a6**
Start file	**aovs-start-1-finish.max**
Final exercise file	**passthrough-finish.max**

Getting Started
Open **aovs-start-1-finish.max** in 3ds Max and make sure **Physical** camera is active.

Working On the Passthrough Shader
Follow these steps:

1. Open **Slate Material Editor**. Disconnect the **mat-chrome** and **AOV Write RGB** nodes.

2. RMB click in the active view and then choose **Materials > Arnold > Utility > Passthrough**; a **Passthrough** node is added to the active view.

3. Connect **mat-chrome** node to the **passthrough** port of the **Passthrough** node. Now, connect **AOV Write RGB** to **eval1** port of the **Passthrough** node. Assign **Passthrough** shader to the bottle in the scene. Fig. E2 shows the node network.

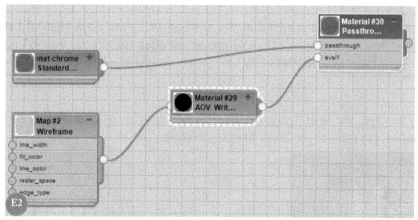

4. RMB click in the active view and then choose **Maps > Arnold > Utility > Utility**; an **Utility** node is added to the active view. In the **Parameter Editor > Utility > Parameters** rollout, change **Color Mode** to **obj** and **Shade Mode** to **flat**.

5. RMB click in the active view and then choose **Materials > Arnold > AOV > AOV Write RGB**; a **AOV Write RGB** node is added to the active view.

6. In the **Parameter Editor > AOV Write RGB > Parameters** rollout, change **AOV Name** to **objPass**. Now, connect **Utility** node to the **aov_input** node of the **AOV Write RGB** node. Next, connect **AOV Write RGB** to **eval2** port of the **Passthrough** node. Fig. E3 shows the node network.

7. Press **F10** to open the **Render Setup** window. In the **AOVs** panel, click **AOVs (EXR) > Add AOV Channel(s) to this EXR file**. Now, change **Enter Custom AOV Name** to **objPass** and then click the **Add to List** button; **objPass** appears under the custom group in the list box.

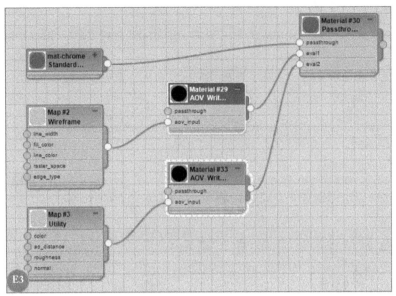

8. Make sure **objPass** is selected in the list box and then click the **Add** button to add **objPass** to the **AOVs (EXR)** group. Render the scene. Fig. E1 shows the **wireframePass** and **objPass** AOVs.

Exercise 3: Working with the Cryptomatte AOVs

In this Exercise, we will work on the **Cryptomatte** AOVs. Fig. E1 show the **crypto_asset**, **crypto_object**, and **crypto_material** AOVs.

Table E3 summarizes the exercise.

Table E3	
Difficulty level	Intermediate
Estimated time to complete	15 Minutes
Topics in exercise	• Getting Started • Working On the Cryptomatte AOVs
Resources folder	**unit-a6**
Start file	**cryptomatte-start.max**
Final exercise file	**cryptomatte-finish.max**

Getting Started
Open **cryptomatte-start.max** in 3ds Max and make sure **Physical** camera is active.

Working On the Cryptomatte AOVs
Follow these steps:

1. Press **F10** to open the **Render Setup** window. In the **AOVs** panel, click **AOVs (EXR) > Add AOV Channel(s) to this EXR file**.

2. Select **crypto_asset, crypto_object,** and **crypto_material** from the **cryptomatte** group and then click the **Add** button to add AOVs to the **AOVs (EXR)** group.

3. In the **AOV Shaders > Maps** group, click one of the **No Map** buttons to open **Material/Map Browser**. Now, double click on **Cryptomatte** in the **Maps > Arnold > Cryptomatte** rollout.

4. Render the scene to view the AOVs [refer to Fig. E1].

Quiz

Multiple Choice
Answer the following questions, only one choice is correct.

1. Which of the following AOVs outputs the alpha channel?

   [A] Alpha   [B] AL
   [C] A   [D] None of these

2. Which of the following AOVs outputs depth of the shading point as seen from the camera?

   [A] Depth   [B] Z Depth
   [C] Z   [D] Camera Depth

3. Which the following Cryptomatte AOVs are available in Arnold?

   [A] crypto_asset   [B] crypto_material
   [C] crypto_object   [D] All of these

Fill in the Blanks

Fill in the blanks in each of the following statements:

1. The _____ AOV outputs direct lighting from all surfaces and volumes.

2. The _____ AOV outputs to RGB with full three-channel opacity (as opposed to single channel alpha).

3. The _____ AOV outputs subsurface scattering and diffuse transmission.

4. _____, an ID matte creation tool created by Jonah Friedman.

True or False

State whether each of the following is true or false:

1. The **shadow_matte** AOV outputs shadows in the scene.

2. The **specular_direct** AOV outputs specular indirect lighting.

3. Multiple shaders in the scene can contribute to the same AOV.

Summary

In this unit, the following topics are covered:

- AOVs
- AOV Settings
- Cryptomatte

Unit PA: Practice Activities [Arnold]

Practice Activities

Activity 1: Creating Metals

Create the Aluminium, Gold, Iron, and Nickel using the **Standard Surface** material. Refer to Figs. A1 through A4.

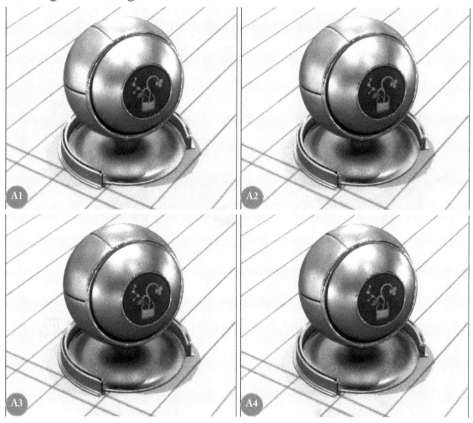

Hint:
*Use the following values for the **Base Color** and **Specular Color** parameters.*

Aluminium:	*0.912, 0.914, 0.920*	*0.970, 0.979, 0.988*
Gold:	*0.944, 0.776, 0.373*	*0.998, 0.981, 0.751*
Iron:	*0.531, 0.512, 0.496*	*0.571, 0.540, 0.586*
Nickel:	*0.649, 0.610, 0.541*	*0.797, 0.801, 0.789*

Activity 2: Creating the Chrome Material

Create the chrome material using the **Standard Surface** shader [see Fig. A5].

Hint:
*Use the white color for both the **Base Color** and **Specular Color** parameters.*

Activity 3: Creating the Glass Material

Create the glass material using the **Standard Surface** shader [see Fig. A6]. Use the **glass-mat-start.max** file.

Hint:
Work on the transmission color and depth to achieve the result.

Activity 4: Creating the Car Paint Material

Create the car paint material using the **Standard Surface** shader [see Figs. A7 and A8].

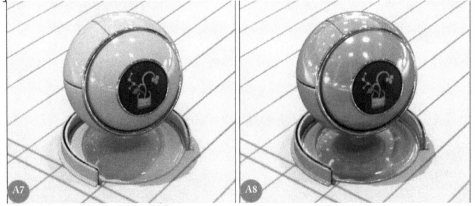

Appendix AA: Quiz Answers [Arnold]

Unit A1 - Introduction to Arnold

Fill in the Blanks
1. Monte Carlo, 2. high-range, 3. raytracing, Sampling, Ray Depth, 4. Camera (AA), 5. Diffuse, 6. Transmission, 7. Specular Ray Depth, 8. Transmission Ray Depth

True/False
1. T, 2. T, 3. F, 4. T, 5. T, 6. F

Unit A2 - Arnold Lights

Multiple Choice
1. B, 2. D

Fill in the Blanks
1. Quad, 2. Spread, 3. Quad X, Quad Y, 4. Diffuse, Specular, SSS, Volume, 5. Physical Sky

True/False
1. T, 2. T, 3. F, 5. F

Unit A3 - Arnold Shaders and Materials

Multiple Choice
1. A, B, 2. A, 3. C, 4. D

Fill in the Blanks
1. ActiveShade, 2. Standard Surface, 3. Base Color, 4. Oren-Nayar, 5. IOR, 6. Depth, 7. SSS, 8. Radius, 9. diffusion, randomwalk, 10. dielectric, 11. Specular IOR, 12. Flake Color, Flakes, 13. Layer, 14. Matte, 15. Base Color, Melanin, 16. Hair and Fur

True/False
1. F, 2. T, 3. T, 4. T, 5. F, 6. F, 7. T, 8. T, 9. F, 10. T, 11. T, 12. T, 13. T, 14. T

Unit A4 - Arnold Maps

Multiple Choice
1. A, C, D. 2. A, B, C

Fill in the Blanks
1. Round Corners, 2. normal, 3. Color Convert, 4. Color Correct, 5. Complement, 6. Multiply, 7. State Vector, 8. Cell Noise, 9. Curvature, 10. Facing Ratio

True/False
1. T, 2. F, 3. T, 4. F, 5. T, 6. T, 7. F, 8. T, 9. F, 10. T

Unit A5 - Cameras

Multiple Choice
1. D, 2. C, 3. D

Fill in the Blanks
1. aperture, 2. Target Distance, 3. Target Distance, 4. Aperture, 5. Duration

True/False
1. T, 2. T, 3. F, 4. T

Unit A6 - Arnold Render Settings

Multiple Choice
1. A, 2. C, 3. D

Fill in the Blanks
1. direct, 2. opacity, 3. sss, 4. Cryptomatte

True/False
1. T, 2. F, 3. T

Index

Other Publications by
PADEXI ACADEMY

*Visit **www.padexi.academy** to know more about the books, eBooks, and video courses published by PADEXI ACADEMY.*

BOOKS

CINEMA 4D

- Exploring 3D Modeling with CINEMA 4D R19
- Exploring MoGraph with CINEMA 4D R19
- Exploring XPresso With CINEMA 4D R19

3ds Max

- Autodesk 3ds Max 2019: Arnold Essentials
- Autodesk 3ds Max 2019: A Detailed Guide to Modeling, Texturing, Lighting, and Rendering
- Exploring 3D Modeling with 3ds Max 2019

Photoshop

- Exploring Filters With Photoshop CC 2017

Courses

CINEMA 4D

- CINEMA 4D XPresso Course - Become a Better CINEMA 4D Artist
- CINEMA 4D XPresso Nodes Reference Library
- 3D Modeling - Spline Modeling Fundamentals in CINEMA 4D
- CINEMA 4D Tutorials Library